AF251888

Justification By Faith: The Doctrine of Gratuitous Justification

John Calvin

Caleb Sinclair

GRAPEVINE INDIA

Published by

GRAPEVINE INDIA PUBLISHERS PVT LTD

www.grapevineindia.com
Delhi | Mumbai
email: grapevineindiapublishers@gmail.com

Ordering Information:
Quantity sales: Special discounts are available on quantity
purchases by corporations, associations, and others.
For details, reach out to the publisher.

Welcome to our Christian book collection!

For access to more Christian audiobooks,

send a blank email to

thegoodchristian10@gmail.com.

Contents

I. Justification by Faith. The Name and Thing Defined.

I think I have already explained, with sufficient care, how that men, being subject to the curse of the law, have no means left of attaining salvation but through faith alone; and also what faith itself is, what Divine blessings it confers on man, and what effects it produces in him. The substance of what I have advanced is, that Christ, being given to us by the goodness of God, is apprehended and possessed by us by faith, by a participation of whom we receive especially two benefits. In the first place, being by his innocence reconciled to God, we have in heaven a propitious father instead of a judge; in the next place, being sanctified by his Spirit, we devote ourselves to innocence and purity of life. Of regeneration, which is the second benefit, I have said what I thought was sufficient. The method of justification has been but slightly touched, because it was necessary, first to understand that the faith, by which alone we attain gratuitous justification through the Divine mercy, is not unattended with good works, and what is the nature of the good works of the saints, in which part of this question consists. The subject of justification, therefore, must now be fully discussed, and discussed with the recollection that it is the principal hinge by which religion is supported, in order that we may apply to it with the greater attention and care. For unless we first of all apprehend in what situation we stand with respect to God, and what his judgment is concerning us, we have no foundation either for a certainty of salvation, or for the exercise of piety towards God. But the necessity of knowing this subject will be more evident from the knowledge itself.

II. But that we may not stumble at the threshold, (which would be the case were we to enter on a disputation concerning a subject not understood by us,) let us first explain the meaning of these expressions. To be justified in the sight of God, To be justified by faith or by works. He is said to be justified in the sight of God who in the Divine judgment is reputed righteous, and accepted on account of his righteousness; for as iniquity is abominable to God, so no sinner can find favour in his sight, as a sinner, or so long as he is considered as such. Wherever sin is, therefore, it is accompanied with the wrath and vengeance of God. He is justified who is considered not as a sinner, but as a righteous person, and on that account stands in safety before the tribunal of God, where all sinners are confounded and ruined. As, if an innocent man be brought under an accusation before the tribunal of a just judge, when judgment is passed according to his innocence, he is said to be justified or acquitted before the judge, so he is justified before God, who, not being numbered among sinners, has God for a witness and asserter of his righteousness. Thus he must be said, therefore, to be justified by works, whose life discovers such purity and holiness, as to deserve the character of righteousness before the throne of God; or who, by the integrity of his works, can answer and satisfy the divine judgment. On the other hand, he will be justified by faith, who, being excluded from the righteousness of works, apprehends by faith the righteousness of Christ, invested in which, he appears, in the sight of God, not as a sinner, but as a righteous man. Thus we simply explain justification to be an acceptance, by which God receives us into his favour, and esteems us as righteous persons; and we say that it consists in the remission of sins and the imputation of the righteousness of Christ.

III. For the confirmation of this point there are many plain testimonies of Scripture. In the first place, that this is the proper and most usual signification of the word, cannot be denied. But since it would be too tedious to collect all the passages and compare them together, let it suffice to have suggested it to the reader; for he will easily observe it of himself. I will only produce a few places, where this justification, which we speak of, is expressly handled. First, where Luke relates that "the people that heard Christ justified God;" and where Christ pronounces that "wisdom is justified of all her children." To justify God, in the former passage, does not signify to confer righteousness, which always remains perfect in him, although the whole world endeavour to rob him of it; nor, in the latter passage, does the justifying of wisdom denote making the doctrine of salvation righteous, which is so of itself; but both passages imply an ascription to God and to his doctrine of the praise which they deserve. Again, when Christ reprehends the Pharisees for "justifying themselves," he does not mean that they attained righteousness by doing what was right, but that they ostentatiously endeavoured to gain the character of righteousness, of which they were destitute. This is better understood by persons who are skilled in the Hebrew language; which gives the appellation of sinners, not only to those who are conscious to themselves of sin, but to persons who fall under a sentence of condemnation. For Bathsheba, when she says, "I and my son Solomon shall be counted offenders," or sinners, confesses no crime, but complains, that she and her son will be exposed to the disgrace of being numbered among condemned criminals. And it appears from the context, that this word, even in the translation, cannot be understood in any other than a relative sense, and that it does not denote the real character. But with respect to the present subject, where Paul says, "The Scripture foresaw that God would justify the heathen through faith," what can we understand, but that God imputes righteousness through faith? Again, when he says that God "justifieth the ungodly which believeth in Jesus," what can be the meaning, but that he delivers him by the blessing of faith from the condemnation deserved by his ungodliness? He speaks still more plainly in the conclusion, when he thus exclaims: "Who shall lay any thing to the charge of God's elect? It is God that justifieth. Who is he that condemneth? It is Christ that died, yea rather, that is risen again, who also maketh intercession for us." For it is just as if he had said, Who shall accuse them whom God absolves? Who shall condemn those for whom Christ intercedes? Justification, therefore, is no other than an acquittal from guilt of him who was accused, as though his innocence had been proved. Since God, therefore, justifies us through the mediation of Christ, he acquits us, not by an admission of our personal innocence, but by an imputation of righteousness; so that we, who are unrighteous in ourselves, are considered as righteous in Christ. This is the doctrine preached by Paul in the thirteenth Chapter of the Acts: "Through this man is preached unto you the forgiveness of sins; and by him all that believe are justified from all things, from which ye could not be justified by the law of Moses." We see that after remission of sins, this justification is mentioned, as if by way of explanation: we see clearly that it means an acquittal; that it is separated from the works of the law; that it is a mere favour of Christ; that it is apprehended by faith: we see, finally, the interposition of a satisfaction, when he says that we are justified from sins by Christ. Thus, when it is said, that the publican "went down to his house justified," we cannot say that he obtained righteousness by any merit of works. The meaning therefore is, that after he had obtained the pardon of his sins, he was considered as righteous in the sight of God. He was righteous, therefore, not through any approbation of his works, but through God's gracious absolution. Wherefore Ambrose beautifully styles confession of sins, a legitimate justification.

IV. But leaving all contention about the term, if we attend to the thing itself, as it is described to us, every doubt will be removed. For Paul certainly describes justification as an acceptance, when he says to the Ephesians, "God hath predestinated us to the adoption of children by Jesus Christ to himself, according to the good pleasure of his will, to the praise of the glory of his grace, wherein he hath made us accepted." The meaning of this passage is the same as when in another place we are said to be "justified freely by his grace." But in the fourth Chapter to the Romans, he first mentions an imputation of righteousness, and immediately represents it as consisting in remission of sins. "David," says he, "describeth the blessedness of the man unto whom God imputeth righteousness without works, saying, Blessed are they whose iniquities are forgiven," &c. He there, indeed, argues not concerning a branch, but the whole of justification. He also adduces the definition of it given by David, when he pronounces them to be blessed who receive the free forgiveness of their sins; whence it appears, that this righteousness of which he speaks is simply opposed to guilt. But the most decisive passage of all on this point, is where he teaches us that the grand object of the ministry of the gospel is, that we may "be reconciled to God," because he is pleased to receive us into his favour through Christ, "not imputing" our "trespasses unto" us. Let the reader carefully examine the whole context; for when, by way of explanation, he just after adds, in order to describe the method of reconciliation, that Christ, "who knew no sin," was "made sin for us," he undoubtedly means by the term "reconciliation," no other than justification. Nor would there be any truth in what he affirms in another place, that we are "made righteous by the obedience of Christ," unless we are reputed righteous before God, in him, and out of ourselves.

V. But since Osiander has introduced I know not what monstrous notion of essential righteousness, by which, though he had no intention to destroy justification by grace, yet he has involved it in such obscurity as darkens pious minds, and deprives them of a serious sense of the grace of Christ,—it will be worth while, before I pass to any thing else, to refute this idle notion. In the first place, this speculation is the mere fruit of insatiable curiosity. He accumulates, indeed, many testimonies of Scripture, to prove that Christ is one with us, and we one with him, of which there is no proof necessary; but for want of observing the bond of this union, he bewilders himself. For us, however, who hold that we are united to Christ by the secret energy of his Spirit, it will be easy to obviate all his sophisms. He had conceived a notion similar to what was held by the Manichæans, so that he wished to transfuse the Divine essence into men. Hence another discovery of his, that Adam was formed in the image of God, because, even antecedently to the fall, Christ had been appointed the exemplar of the human nature. But for the sake of brevity, I shall only insist on the subject now before us. He says that we are one with Christ. This we admit; but we at the same time deny that Christ's essence is blended with ours. In the next place, we assert that this principle—that Christ is our righteousness because he is the eternal God, the fountain of righteousness, and the essential righteousness of God—is grossly perverted to support his fallacies. The reader will excuse me, if I now just hint at these things, which the order of the treatise requires to be deferred to another place. But though he alleges, in vindication of himself, that by the term essential righteousness he only intends to oppose the opinion that we are reputed righteous for the sake of Christ, yet he manifestly shows, that, not content with that righteousness which has been procured for us by the obedience and sacrificial death of Christ, he imagines that we are substantially righteous in God, by the infusion of his essence as well as his character. For this is the reason why he so vehemently contends, that not only Christ, but the Father and the Holy Spirit also dwell in us; which, though I allow it to be a truth, yet I maintain that he has grossly perverted. For he ought to have fully considered the nature of this inhabitation; namely, that the Father and the Spirit are in Christ; and that as "all the fulness of the Godhead dwelleth in him," so in him we possess the whole Deity. Whatever, therefore, he advances concerning the Father and the Spirit separately, has no other tendency but to seduce the simple from Christ. In the next place, he introduces a mixture of substances, by which God, transfusing himself into us, makes us, as it were, a part of himself. For he considers it as of no importance, that the power of the Holy Spirit unites us to Christ, so that he becomes our head and we become his members, unless his essence be blended with ours. But when speaking of the Father and the Spirit, he more openly betrays his opinion; which is, that we are not justified by the sole grace of the Mediator, and that righteousness is not simply or really offered to us in his person; but that we are made partakers of the Divine righteousness when God is essentially united with us.

VI. If he had only said, that Christ in justifying us becomes ours by an essential union, and that he is our head not only as man, but that the essence of his Divine nature also is infused into us,—he might have entertained himself with his fancies with less mischief, nor perhaps would so great a contention have been excited about this reverie. But as this principle is like a cuttlefish, which, by the emission of black and turbid blood, conceals its many tails, there is a necessity for a vigorous opposition to it, unless we mean to submit to be openly robbed of that righteousness which alone affords us any confidence concerning our salvation. For throughout this discussion, the terms righteousness and justify are extended by him to two things. First, he understands that "to be justified" denotes not only to be reconciled to God by a free pardon, but also to be made righteous; and that righteousness is not a gratuitous imputation, but a sanctity and integrity inspired by the Divine essence which resides in us. Secondly, he resolutely denies that Christ is our righteousness, as having, in the character of a priest, expiated our sins and appeased the Father on our behalf, but as being the eternal God and everlasting life. To prove the first assertion, that God justifies not only by pardoning, but also by regenerating, he inquires whether God leaves those whom he justifies in their natural state, without any reformation of their manners. The answer is very easy; as Christ cannot be divided, so these two blessings, which we receive together in him, are also inseparable. Whomsoever, therefore, God receives into his favour, he likewise gives them the Spirit of adoption, by whose power he renews them in his own image. But if the brightness of the sun be inseparable from his heat, shall we therefore say that the earth is warmed by his light, and illuminated by his heat? Nothing can be more apposite to the present subject than this similitude. The beams of the sun quicken and fertilize the earth, his rays brighten and illuminate it. Here is a mutual and indivisible connection. Yet reason itself prohibits us to transfer to one what is peculiar to the other. In this confusion of two blessings which Osiander obtrudes on us, there is a similar absurdity. For as God actually renews to the practice of righteousness those whom he gratuitously accepts as righteous, Osiander confounds that gift of regeneration with this gracious acceptance, and contends that they are one and the same. But the Scripture, though it connects them together, yet enumerates them distinctly, that the manifold grace of God may be the more evident to us. For that passage of Paul is not superfluous, that "Christ is made unto us righteousness and sanctification." And whenever he argues, from the salvation procured for us, from the paternal love of God, and from the grace of Christ, that we are called to holiness and purity, he plainly indicates that it is one thing to be justified, and another thing to be made new creatures. When Osiander appeals to the Scripture, he corrupts as many passages as he cites. The assertion of Paul, that "to him that worketh not, but believeth on him that justifieth the ungodly, his faith is counted for righteousness," is explained by Osiander to denote making a man righteous. With the same temerity he corrupts the whole of that fourth Chapter to the Romans, and hesitates not to impose the same false gloss on the passage just cited, "Who shall lay any thing to the charge of God's elect? It is God that justifieth;" where it is evident that the apostle is treating simply of accusation and absolution, and that his meaning wholly rests on the antithesis. His folly, therefore, betrays itself both in his arguments and in his citations of Scripture proofs. With no more propriety does he treat of the word righteousness, when he says, "that faith was reckoned to Abraham for righteousness," because that after having embraced Christ, (who is the righteousness of God, and God himself,) he was eminent for the greatest virtues. Whence it appears, that of two good parts, he erroneously makes one corrupt whole; for the righteousness there mentioned does not belong to the whole course of Abraham's life; but rather the Spirit testifies that, notwithstanding the singular eminence of Abraham's virtues, and his laudable and persevering advancement in them, yet he did not please God any otherwise than in receiving by faith the grace offered in the promise. Whence it follows, that in justification there is no regard paid to works, as Paul conclusively argues in that passage.

VII. His objection, that the power of justifying belongs not to faith of itself, but only as it receives Christ, I readily admit. For if faith were to justify of itself, or by an intrinsic efficacy, as it is expressed, being always weak and imperfect, it never could effect this but in part; and thus it would be a defective justification, which would only confer on us a partial salvation. Now, we entertain no such notion as the objection supposes; on the contrary, we affirm that, strictly speaking, "it is God that justifies;" and then we transfer this to Christ, because he is given to us for righteousness. Faith we compare to a vessel; for unless we come empty with the mouth of our soul open to implore the grace of Christ, we cannot receive Christ. Whence it may be inferred, that we do not detract from Christ the power of justifying, when we teach that faith receives him before it receives his righteousness. Nevertheless, I cannot admit the intricate comparisons of this sophist, when he says that faith is Christ; as though an earthen vessel were a treasure, because gold is concealed in it. For faith, although intrinsically it is of no dignity or value, justifies us by an application of Christ, just as a vessel full of money constitutes a man rich. Therefore I maintain that faith, which is only the instrument by which righteousness is received, cannot without absurdity be confounded with Christ, who is the material cause, and at once the author and dispenser of so great a benefit. We have now removed the difficulty as to the sense in which the word faith ought to be understood, when it is applied to justification.

VIII. Respecting the reception of Christ, he goes still greater lengths; asserting that the internal word is received by the ministry of the external word, by which he would divert us from the priesthood of Christ and the person of the Mediator, to his eternal divinity. We do not divide Christ, but we maintain that the same person, who, by reconciling us to the Father in his own flesh, has given us righteousness, is the eternal Word of God; and we confess that he could not otherwise have discharged the office of Mediator, and procured righteousness for us, if he were not the eternal God. But the opinion of Osiander is, that since Christ is both God and man, he is made righteousness to us, in respect of his Divine, not his human nature. Now, if this properly belong to the Divinity, it will not be peculiar to Christ, but common also to the Father and the Spirit; since the righteousness of one is the same as that of the others. Besides, what has been naturally eternal, cannot with propriety be said to be "made unto us." But though we grant that God is made righteousness unto us, how will it agree with the clause which is inserted, that "of God," he "is made unto us righteousness?" This is certainly peculiar to the character of the Mediator, who, though he contains in himself the Divine nature, yet is designated by this appropriate title, by which he is distinguished from the Father and the Spirit. But he ridiculously triumphs in that single expression of Jeremiah, where he promises that "the Lord," Jehovah, will be "our righteousness." He can deduce nothing from this, but that Christ, who is our righteousness, is God manifested in the flesh. We have elsewhere recited from Paul's sermon, that "God hath purchased the Church with his own blood." If any should infer from this, that the blood by which our sins were expiated, was Divine, and part of the Divine nature, who could bear so monstrous an error? But Osiander thinks he has gained every thing by this very puerile cavil; he swells, exults, and fills many pages with his swelling words, though the passage is simply and readily explained, by saying that Jehovah, when he should become the seed of David, would be the righteousness of the pious; and in the same sense Isaiah informs us, "by his knowledge shall my righteous servant justify many." Let us remark, that the speaker here is the Father; that he attributes to his Son the office of justifying; that he adds as a reason, that he is righteous; and that he places the mode or means of effecting this, in the doctrine by which Christ is made known. For it is more suitable to understand the word תעד in a passive sense. Hence I conclude, first, that Christ was made righteousness when he assumed the form of a servant; secondly, that he justifies us by his own obedience to the Father; and, therefore, that he does this for us, not according to his Divine nature, but by reason of the dispensation committed to him. For though God alone is the fountain of righteousness, and we are righteous only by a participation of him, yet, because we have been alienated from his righteousness through the unhappy breach occasioned by the fall, we are under the necessity of descending to this inferior remedy, to be justified by Christ, by the efficacy of his death and resurrection.

IX. If Osiander object, that the excellence of this work surpasses the nature of man, and therefore can be ascribed only to the Divine nature,—the former part of the objection I admit, but in the latter I maintain that he is grossly mistaken. For although Christ could neither purify our souls with his blood, nor appease the Father by his sacrifice, nor absolve us from guilt, nor, in short, perform the functions of a priest, if he were not truly God, because human power would have been unequal to so great a burden, yet it is certain that he performed all these things in his human nature. For if it be inquired, How are we justified? Paul replies, "By the obedience" of Christ. But has he obeyed in any other way than by assuming the form of a servant? Hence we infer, that righteousness is presented to us in his flesh. In the other passage also, which I much wonder that Osiander is not ashamed to quote so frequently, Paul places the source of righteousness wholly in the humanity of Christ. "He hath made him to be sin for us, who knew no sin, that we might be made the righteousness of God in him." Osiander lays great stress on "the righteousness of God," and triumphs as though he had evinced it to be his notion of essential righteousness; whereas the words convey a very different idea,—that we are righteous through the expiation effected by Christ. That "the righteousness of God" means that which God approves, ought to have been known to the youngest novices; just as in John "the praise of God" is opposed to "the praise of men." I know that "the righteousness of God" sometimes denotes that of which he is the author, and which he bestows upon us; but, without any observation of mine, the judicious reader will perceive that the meaning of this passage is only, that we stand before the tribunal of God supported by the atoning death of Christ. Nor is the term of such great importance, provided that Osiander coincides with us in this, that we are justified in Christ, inasmuch as he was made an expiatory sacrifice for us; which is altogether incompatible with his Divine nature. For this reason, when Christ designs to seal the righteousness and salvation which he has presented to us, he exhibits a certain pledge of it in his flesh. He calls himself, indeed, "living bread;" but adds, by way of explanation, "my flesh is meat indeed, and my blood is drink indeed." This method of instruction is discovered in the sacraments; which, although they direct our faith to the whole of the person of Christ, not to a part of him only, yet at the same time teach that the matter of justification and salvation resides in his human nature; not that he either justifies or vivifies, of himself as a mere man, but because it has pleased God to manifest in the Mediator that which was incomprehensible and hidden in himself. Wherefore I am accustomed to say, that Christ is, as it were, a fountain opened to us, whence we may draw what were otherwise concealed and useless in that secret and deep fountain which flows to us in the person of the Mediator. In this manner, and in this sense, provided he will submit to the clear and forcible arguments which I have adduced, I do not deny that Christ justifies us, as he is God and man, and that this work is common also to the Father and the Spirit; and, finally, that the righteousness of which Christ makes us partakers, is the eternal righteousness of the eternal God.

X. Moreover, that his cavils may not deceive the inexperienced, I confess that we are destitute of this incomparable blessing, till Christ becomes ours. I attribute, therefore, the highest importance to the connection between the head and members; to the inhabitation of Christ in our hearts; in a word, to the mystical union by which we enjoy him, so that being made ours, he makes us partakers of the blessings with which he is furnished. We do not, then, contemplate him at a distance out of ourselves, that his righteousness may be imputed to us; but because we have put him on, and are ingrafted into his body, and because he has deigned to unite us to himself, therefore we glory in a participation of his righteousness. Thus we refute the cavil of Osiander, that faith is considered by us as righteousness; as though we despoiled Christ of his right, when we affirm, that by faith we come to him empty, that he alone may fill us with his grace. But Osiander, despising this spiritual connection, insists on a gross mixture of Christ with believers; and therefore invidiously gives the appellation of Zuinglians to all who do not subscribe to his fanatical error concerning essential righteousness; because they are not of opinion that Christ is substantially eaten in the sacred supper. As for myself, indeed, I consider it the highest honour to be thus reproached by a man so proud and so absorbed in his own delusions; although he attacks not me alone, but other writers well known in the world, whom he ought to have treated with modest respect. But this does not at all affect me, who am supporting no private interest; wherefore I the more unreservedly advocate this cause, conscious that I am free from every sinister motive. His great importunity in insisting on essential righteousness, and an essential inhabitation of Christ in us, goes to this length—first, that God transfuses himself into us by a gross mixture of himself with us, as he pretends that there is a carnal eating in the sacred supper; secondly, that God inspires his righteousness into us, by which we are really righteous with him, since, according to this man, such righteousness is as really God himself, as the goodness, or holiness, or perfection of God. I shall not take much trouble to refute the testimonies adduced by him, which he violently perverts from the celestial to the present state. By Christ, says Peter, "are given unto us exceeding great and precious promises; that by these ye might be partakers of the Divine nature." As though we were now such as the gospel promises we shall be at the second advent of Christ; nay, John apprizes us, that then "we shall be like God; for we shall see him as he is." I have thought proper to give the reader only a small specimen, and endeavoured to pass over these impertinences, not that it is difficult to refute them, but because I am unwilling to be tedious in labouring to no purpose.

XI. There is yet more latent poison in the second particular, in which he maintains, that we are righteous together with God. I think I have already sufficiently demonstrated, that although this dogma were not so pestiferous, yet because it is weak and unsatisfactory, and evaporates through its own inanity, it ought justly to be rejected by all judicious and pious readers. But this is an impiety not to be tolerated—under the pretext of a twofold righteousness to weaken the assurance of salvation, and to elevate us above the clouds, that we may not embrace by faith the grace of expiation, and call upon God with tranquillity of mind. Osiander ridicules those who say that justification is a forensic term, because it is necessary for us to be actually righteous: nor is there any thing that he more dislikes than the doctrine that we are justified by gratuitous imputation. Now, if God do not justify by absolving and pardoning us, what is the meaning of this declaration of Paul? "God was in Christ, reconciling the world unto himself, not imputing their trespasses unto them. For he hath made him to be sin for us, who knew no sin; that we might be made the righteousness of God in him." First I find, that they are accounted righteous who are reconciled to God: the manner is specified, that God justifies by pardoning; just as, in another passage, justification is opposed to accusation; which antithesis clearly demonstrates, that the form of expression is borrowed from the practice of courts. Nor is there any one, but tolerably versed in the Hebrew language, provided at the same time that he be in his sound senses, who can be ignorant that this is the original of the phrase, and that this is its import and meaning. Now, let Osiander answer me whether, where Paul says that "David describeth righteousness without works, saying, Blessed are they whose iniquities are forgiven," whether, I say, this be a complete definition or a partial one. Certainly Paul does not adduce the testimony of the Psalmist, as teaching that pardon of sins is a part of righteousness, or concurs to the justification of a man; but he includes the whole of righteousness in a free remission, pronouncing, "Blessed are they whose iniquities are forgiven, and whose sins are covered. Blessed is the man to whom the Lord will not impute sin." He thence estimates and judges of the felicity of such a man, because in this way he becomes righteous, not actually, but by imputation. Osiander objects, that it would be dishonourable to God, and contrary to his nature, if he justified those who still remain actually impious. But it should be remembered that, as I have already observed, the grace of justification is inseparable from regeneration, although they are distinct things. But since it is sufficiently known from experience, that some relics of sin always remain in the righteous, the manner of their justification must of necessity be very different from that of their renovation to newness of life. For the latter God commences in his elect, and as long as they live carries it on gradually, and sometimes slowly, so that they are always obnoxious at his tribunal to the sentence of death. He justifies them, however, not in a partial manner, but so completely, that they may boldly appear in heaven, as being invested with the purity of Christ. For no portion of righteousness could satisfy our consciences, till we have ascertained that God is pleased with us, as being unexceptionably righteous before him. Whence it follows, that the doctrine of justification is perverted and totally overturned, when doubts are injected into the mind, when the confidence of salvation is shaken, when bold and fearless worship is interrupted, and when quiet and tranquillity with spiritual joy are not established. Whence Paul argues from the incompatibility of things contrary to each other, that the inheritance is not of the law, because then faith would be rendered vain; which, if it be fixed upon works, must inevitably fall; since not even the most holy of all saints will find them afford any ground of confidence. This difference between justification and regeneration (which Osiander confounds together, and denominates a twofold righteousness) is beautifully expressed by Paul; for, speaking of his real righteousness, or of the integrity which he possessed, to which Osiander gives the appellation of essential righteousness, he sorrowfully exclaims, "O wretched man that I am! who shall deliver me from the body of this death?" But resorting to the righteousness which is founded in the Divine mercy alone, he nobly triumphs over life, and death, and reproaches, and famine, and the sword, and all adverse things and persons. "Who shall lay any thing to the charge of God's elect? It is God that justifieth. For I am persuaded, that nothing shall be able to separate us from the love of God, which is in Christ Jesus our Lord." He plainly declares himself to be possessed of that righteousness, which alone is fully sufficient for salvation in the sight of God; so that the miserable servitude, in a consciousness of which he was just before bewailing his condition, neither diminishes, nor in the smallest degree interrupts, the confidence with which he triumphs. This diversity is sufficiently known, and is even familiar to all the saints, who groan under the burden of their iniquities, and yet with victorious confidence rise superior to every fear. But the objection of Osiander, that it is incongruous to the nature of God, recoils upon himself; for, although he invests the saints with a twofold righteousness, as with a garment covered with skins, he is, notwithstanding, constrained to acknowledge that no man can please God without the remission of his sins. If this be true, he should at least grant that they who are not actually righteous, are accounted righteous in proportion, as it is expressed, to the degree of imputation. But how far shall a sinner extend this gracious acceptance, which is substituted in the place of righteousness? Shall he estimate it by the weight? Truly he will be in great uncertainty to which side to incline the balance; because he will not be able to assume to himself as much righteousness as may be necessary to his confidence. It is well that he, who would wish to prescribe laws to God, is not the arbiter of this cause. But this address of David to God will remain: "That thou mightest be justified when thou speakest, and be clear when thou judgest." And what extreme arrogance it is to condemn the supreme Judge when he freely absolves, and not to be satisfied with this answer, "I will show mercy on whom I will show mercy!" And yet the intercession of Moses, which God checked with this reply, was not that he would spare none, but that, though they were guilty, he would remove their guilt and absolve them all at once. We affirm, therefore, that those who were undone are justified before God by the obliteration of their sins; because, sin being the object of his hatred, he can love none but those whom he justifies. But this is a wonderful method of justification, that sinners, being invested with the righteousness of Christ, dread not the judgment which they have deserved; and that, while they justly condemn themselves, they are accounted righteous out of themselves.

XII. But the readers must be cautioned to pay a strict attention to the mystery which Osiander boasts that he will not conceal from them. For, after having contended with great prolixity, that we do not obtain favour with God solely through the imputation of the righteousness of Christ, because it would be impossible for him to esteem those as righteous who are not so, (I use his own words,) he at length concludes, that Christ is given to us for righteousness, not in respect of his human, but of his Divine nature; and that, though this righteousness can only be found in the person of the Mediator, yet it is the righteousness, not of man, but of God. He does not combine two righteousnesses, but evidently deprives the humanity of Christ of all concern in the matter of justification. It is worth while, however, to hear what arguments he adduces. It is said in the passage referred to, that "Christ is made unto us wisdom," which is applicable only to the eternal Word. Neither, therefore, is Christ, considered as man our righteousness. I reply, that the only begotten Son of God was indeed his eternal wisdom; but this title is here ascribed to him by Paul in a different sense, because "in him are hid all the treasures of wisdom and knowledge." What, therefore, he had with the Father, he has manifested to us; and so what Paul says, refers not to the essence of the Son of God, but to our benefit, and is rightly applied to the humanity of Christ; because, although he was a light shining in darkness before his assumption of the flesh, yet he was a hidden light till he appeared in the nature of man "as the Sun of righteousness;" wherefore he calls himself "the light of the world." Osiander betrays his folly likewise in objecting, that justification exceeds the power of angels and men; since it depends not upon the dignity of any creature, but upon the appointment of God. If angels were desirous to offer a satisfaction to God, it would be unavailing; because they have not been appointed to it. This was peculiar to the man Christ, who was "made under the law, to redeem us from the curse of the law." He likewise very unjustly accuses those who deny that Christ is our righteousness according to his Divine nature, of retaining only one part of Christ, and (what is worse) making two Gods; because, though they acknowledge that God dwells in us, yet they flatly deny that we are righteous through the righteousness of God. For if we call Christ the author of life in consequence of his having suffered death, "that he might destroy him that had the power of death," it is not to be inferred that we deny this honour to his complete person, as God manifested in the flesh: we only state with precision the means by which the righteousness of God is conveyed to us, so that we may enjoy it. In this, Osiander has fallen into a very pernicious error. We do not deny, that what is openly exhibited to us in Christ flows from the secret grace and power of God; nor do we refuse to admit, that the righteousness conferred on us by Christ is the righteousness of God as proceeding from him; but we constantly maintain that we have righteousness and life in the death and resurrection of Christ. I pass over that shameful accumulation of passages, with which, without any discrimination, and even without common sense, he has burdened the reader, in order to evince, that wherever mention is made of righteousness, it ought to be understood of this essential righteousness; as where David implores the righteousness of God to assist him; which as he does above a hundred times, Osiander hesitates not to pervert such a great number of passages. Nor is there any thing more solid in his other objection, that the term "righteousness" is properly and rightly applied to that by which we are excited to rectitude of conduct, and that God alone "worketh in us both to will and to do." Now, we do not deny, that God renews us by his Spirit to holiness and righteousness of life; but it should first be inquired, whether he does this immediately by himself, or through the medium of his Son, with whom he has deposited all the plenitude of his Spirit, that with his abundance he might relieve the necessities of his members. Besides, though righteousness flows to us from the secret fountain of the Divinity, yet it does not follow that Christ, who in the flesh sanctified himself for our sakes, is our righteousness with respect to his Divine nature. Equally frivolous is his assertion, that Christ himself was righteous with the righteousness of God; because, if he had not been influenced by the will of the Father, not even he could have performed the part assigned him. For though it has been elsewhere observed, that all the merit of Christ himself flows from the mere favour of God, yet this affords no countenance to the fanciful notion with which Osiander fascinates his own eyes and those of the injudicious. For who would admit the inference, that because God is the original source of our righteousness, we are therefore essentially righteous, and have the essence of the Divine righteousness residing in us? In redeeming the Church (Isaiah says) God "put on righteousness as a breastplate;" but was it to spoil Christ of the armour which he had given him, and to prevent his being a perfect Redeemer? The prophet only meant that God borrowed nothing extrinsic to himself, and had no assistance in the work of our redemption. Paul has briefly intimated the same in other words, saying that he has given us salvation in order "to declare his righteousness." Nor does this at all contradict what he states in another place, "that by the obedience of one we are made righteous." To conclude: whoever fabricates a twofold righteousness, that wretched souls may not rely wholly and exclusively on the Divine mercy, makes Christ an object of contempt, and crowns him with platted thorns.

XIII. But as many persons imagine righteousness to be composed of faith and works, let us also prove, before we proceed, that the righteousness of faith is so exceedingly different from that of works, that if one be established, the other must necessarily be subverted. The apostle says, "I count all things but dung, that I may win Christ, and be found in him, not having mine own righteousness, which is of the law, but that which is through the faith of Christ, the righteousness which is of God by faith." Here we see a comparison of two opposites, and an implication that his own righteousness must be forsaken by him who wishes to obtain the righteousness of Christ. Wherefore, in another place, he states this to have been the cause of the ruin of the Jews, that, "going about to establish their own righteousness, they have not submitted themselves unto the righteousness of God." If, by establishing our own righteousness, we reject the righteousness of God, then, in order to obtain the latter, the former must doubtless be entirely renounced. He conveys the same sentiment when he asserts, that "boasting is excluded. By what law? of works? Nay; but by the law of faith." Whence it follows, that as long as there remains the least particle of righteousness in our works, we retain some cause for boasting. But if faith excludes all boasting, the righteousness of works can by no means be associated with the righteousness of faith. To this purpose he speaks so clearly in the fourth Chapter to the Romans, as to leave no room for cavil or evasion. "If Abraham (says he) were justified by works, he hath whereof to glory." He adds, "but" he hath "not" whereof to glory "before God." It follows, therefore, that he was not justified by works. Then he advances another argument from two opposites. "To him that worketh is the reward not reckoned of grace, but of debt." But righteousness is attributed to faith through grace. Therefore it is not from the merit of works. Adieu, therefore, to the fanciful notion of those who imagine a righteousness compounded of faith and works.

XIV. The sophists, who amuse and delight themselves with perversion of the Scripture and vain cavils, think they have found a most excellent subterfuge, when they explain works, in these passages, to mean those which men yet unregenerate perform without the grace of Christ, merely through the unassisted efforts of their own free-will; and deny that they relate to spiritual works. Thus, according to them, a man is justified both by faith and by works, only the works are not properly his own, but the gifts of Christ and the fruits of regeneration. For they say that Paul spoke in this manner, only that the Jews, who relied on their own strength, might be convinced of their folly in arrogating righteousness to themselves, whereas it is conferred on us solely by the Spirit of Christ, not by any exertion properly our own. But they do not observe, that in the contrast of legal and evangelical righteousness, which Paul introduces in another place, all works are excluded, by what title soever they may be distinguished. For he teaches that this is the righteousness of the law, that he who has fulfilled the command of the law shall obtain salvation; but that the righteousness of faith consists in believing that Christ has died and is risen again. Besides, we shall see, as we proceed, in its proper place, that sanctification and righteousness are separate blessings of Christ. Whence it follows, that even spiritual works are not taken into the account, when the power of justifying is attributed to faith. And the assertion of Paul, in the place just cited, that Abraham has not whereof to glory before God, since he was not justified by works, ought not to be restricted to any literal appearance or external display of virtue, or to any efforts of free-will; but though the life of the patriarch was spiritual, and almost angelic, yet his works did not possess sufficient merit to justify him before God.

XV. The errors of the schoolmen, who mingle their preparations, are rather more gross; but they instil into the simple and incautious a doctrine equally corrupt, while under the pretext of the Spirit and of grace, they conceal the mercy of God, which alone can calm the terrors of the conscience. We confess, indeed, with Paul, that "the doers of the law are justified before God;" but since we are all far from being observers of the law, we conclude, that those works which should be principally available to justification, afford us no assistance, because we are destitute of them. With respect to the common Papists, or schoolmen, they are in this matter doubly deceived; both in denominating faith a certainty of conscience in expecting from God a reward of merit, and in explaining the grace of God to be, not an imputation of gratuitous righteousness, but the Spirit assisting to the pursuit of holiness. They read in the apostle, "He that cometh to God must believe that he is, and that he is a rewarder of them that diligently seek him." But they do not consider the manner of seeking him. And that they mistake the sense of the word "grace," is evident from their writings. For Lombard represents justification by Christ as given us in two ways. He says, "The death of Christ justifies us, first, because it excites charity in our hearts, by which we are made actually righteous;

secondly, because it destroys sin, by which the devil held us in captivity, so that now it cannot condemn us." We see how he considers the grace of God in justification to consist in our being directed to good works by the grace of the Holy Spirit. He wished, indeed, to follow the opinion of Augustine; but he follows him at a great distance, and even deviates considerably from a close imitation of him; for whatever he finds clearly stated by him, he obscures, and whatever he finds pure in him, he corrupts. The schools have always been running into worse and worse errors, till at length they have precipitated themselves into a kind of Pelagianism. Nor, indeed, is the opinion of Augustine, or at least his manner of expression, to be altogether admitted. For though he excellently despoils man of all the praise of righteousness, and ascribes the whole to the grace of God, yet he refers grace to sanctification, in which we are regenerated by the Spirit to newness of life.

XVI. The Scripture, when speaking of the righteousness of faith, leads us to something very different. It teaches us, that being diverted from the contemplation of our own works, we should regard nothing but the mercy of God and the perfection of Christ. For it states this to be the order of justification; that from the beginning God deigns to embrace sinful man with his pure and gratuitous goodness, contemplating nothing in him to excite mercy, but his misery; (for God beholds him utterly destitute of all good works;) deriving from himself the motive for blessing him, that he may affect the sinner himself with a sense of his supreme goodness, who, losing all confidence in his own works, rests the whole of his salvation on the Divine mercy. This is the sentiment of faith, by which the sinner comes to the enjoyment of his salvation, when he knows from the doctrine of the gospel that he is reconciled to God; that having obtained remission of sins, he is justified by the intervention of the righteousness of Christ; and though regenerated by the Spirit of God, he thinks on everlasting righteousness reserved for him, not in the good works to which he devotes himself, but solely in the righteousness of Christ. When all these things shall have been particularly examined, they will afford a perspicuous explication of our opinion. They will, however, be better digested in a different order from that in which they have been proposed. But it is of little importance, provided they are so connected with each other, that we may have the whole subject rightly stated and well confirmed.

XVII. Here it is proper to recall to remembrance the relation we have before stated between faith and the gospel; since the reason why faith is said to justify, is, that it receives and embraces the righteousness offered in the gospel. But its being offered by the gospel absolutely excludes all consideration of works. This Paul very clearly demonstrates on various occasions; and particularly in two passages. In his Epistle to the Romans, contrasting the law and the gospel, he says, "Moses describeth the righteousness which is of the law, that the man which doeth those things shall live by them. But the righteousness which is of faith speaketh on this wise: That if thou shalt confess with thy mouth the Lord Jesus, and shalt believe in thine heart that God hath raised him from the dead, thou shalt be saved." Do you perceive how he thus discriminates between the law and the gospel, that the former attributes righteousness to works, but the latter bestows it freely, without the assistance of works? It is a remarkable passage, and may serve to extricate us from a multitude of difficulties, if we understand that the righteousness which is given us by the gospel is free from all legal conditions. This is the reason why he more than once strongly opposes the promise to the law. "If the inheritance be of the law, it is no more of promise;" and more in the same Chapter to the same purpose. It is certain that the law also has its promises. Wherefore, unless we will confess the comparison to be improper, there must be something distinct and different in the promises of the gospel. Now, what can that be, but that they are gratuitous and solely dependent on the Divine mercy, whilst the promises of the law depend on the condition of works? Nor let any one object, that it is only the righteousness which men would obtrude on God from their own natural powers and free-will that is rejected; since Paul teaches it as a universal truth, that the precepts of the law are unprofitable, because, not only among the vulgar, but even among the very best of men, there is not one who can fulfil them. Love is certainly the principal branch of the law: when the Spirit of God forms us to it, why does it not constitute any part of our righteousness, but because even in the saints it is imperfect, and therefore of itself deserves no reward?

XVIII. The other passage is as follows: "That no man is justified by the law in the sight of God, it is evident; for, The just shall live by faith. And the law is not of faith; but, The man that doeth them shall live in them." How could this argument be supported, unless it were certain that works do not come into the account of faith, but are to be entirely separated from it? The law, he says, differs from faith. Why? Because works are required to the righteousness of the law. It follows, therefore, that works are not required to the righteousness of faith. From this statement it appears, that they who are justified by faith, are justified without the merit of works, and beyond the merit of works; for faith receives that righteousness which the gospel bestows; and the gospel differs from the law in this respect, that it does not confine righteousness to works, but rests it entirely on the mercy of God. He argues in a similar manner to the Romans, that "Abraham had not whereof to glory; for he believed God, and it was counted unto him for righteousness;" and by way of confirmation he subjoins, that then there is room for the righteousness of faith when there are no works which merit any reward. He tells us, that where there are works, they receive a reward "of debt," but that what is given to faith is "of grace;" for this is the clear import of the language which he there uses. When he adds, a little after, "Therefore it is of faith" that we obtain the inheritance, in order "that it might be by grace," he infers that the inheritance is gratuitous, because it is received by faith: and why is this, but because faith, without any assistance of works, depends wholly on the Divine mercy? And in the same sense undoubtedly he elsewhere teaches us, that "the righteousness of God without the law is manifested, being witnessed by the law and the prophets;" because, by excluding the law, he denies that righteousness is assisted by works, or that we obtain it by working, but asserts that we come empty in order to receive it.

XIX. The reader will now discover, with what justice the sophists of the present day cavil at our doctrine, when we say that a man is justified by faith only. That a man is justified by faith, they do not deny, because the Scripture so often declares it; but since it is nowhere expressly said to be by faith only, they cannot bear this addition to be made. But what reply will they give to these words of Paul, where he contends that "righteousness is not of faith unless it be gratuitous?" How can any thing gratuitous consist with works? And by what cavils will they elude what he asserts in another place, that in the gospel "is the righteousness of God revealed?" If righteousness is revealed in the gospel, it is certainly not a mutilated and partial, but a complete and perfect one. The law, therefore, has no concern in it. And respecting this exclusive particle, only, they rest on an evasion which is not only false, but glaringly ridiculous. For does not he most completely attribute every thing to faith alone, who denies every thing to works? What is the meaning of these expressions of Paul? "Righteousness is manifested without the law," "justified freely by his grace," "justified without the deeds of the law." Here they have an ingenious subterfuge, which, though it is not of their own invention, but borrowed from Origen and some of the ancients, is nevertheless very absurd. They pretend that the works excluded are the ceremonial works of the law, not the moral works. They have made such a proficiency by their perpetual disputations, that they have forgotten the first elements of logic. Do they suppose the apostle to have been insane, when he adduced these passages in proof of his doctrine? "The man that doeth them shall live in them;" and "Cursed is every one that continueth not in all things which are written in the book of the law to do them." If they be in their sober senses, they will not assert that life was promised to the observers of ceremonies, and the curse denounced merely on the transgressors of them. If these places are to be understood of the moral law, it is beyond a doubt, that moral works likewise are excluded from the power to justify. To the same purpose are these arguments which he uses: "For by the law is the knowledge of sin;" consequently not righteousness. "Because the law worketh wrath," therefore not righteousness. Since the law cannot assure our consciences, neither can it confer righteousness. Since faith is counted for righteousness, consequently righteousness is not a reward of works, but is gratuitously bestowed. Since we are justified by faith, boasting is precluded. "If there had been a law given which could have given life, verily righteousness should have been by the law. But the Scripture hath concluded all under sin, that the promise by faith of Jesus Christ might be given to them that believe." Let them idly pretend, if they dare, that these are applicable to ceremonies, not to morals; but even children would explode such consummate impudence. We may therefore be assured, that when the power of justifying is denied to the law, the whole law is included.

XX. If any one should wonder why the apostle does not content himself with simply mentioning works, but says works of the law, the reason is obvious. For though works are so greatly esteemed, they derive their value from the Divine approbation rather than from any intrinsic excellence. For who can dare to boast to God of any righteousness of works, but what he has approved? Who can dare to claim any reward as due to them, but what he has promised? It is owing, therefore, to the Divine favour, that they are accounted worthy both of the title and of the reward of righteousness; and so they are valuable, only when they are intended as acts of obedience to God. Wherefore the apostle, in another place, in order to prove that Abraham could not be justified by works, alleges, that "the law was four hundred and thirty years after the covenant was confirmed." Ignorant persons would ridicule such an argument, because there might have been righteous works before the promulgation of the law; but knowing that works have no such intrinsic worth, independently of the testimony and esteem of God, he has taken it for granted that, antecedently to the law, they had no power to justify. We know why he expressly mentions "the works of the law," when he means to deny justification by works; it is because they alone can furnish any occasion of controversy. However, he likewise excludes all works, without any limitation, as when he says, "David describeth the blessedness of the man, unto whom God imputeth righteousness without works." They cannot, therefore, by any subtleties prevent us from retaining this general exclusive particle. It is in vain, also, that they catch at another frivolous subtlety, alleging that we are justified only by that "faith which worketh by love;" with a view to represent righteousness as depending on love. We acknowledge, indeed, with Paul, that no other faith justifies, except that "which worketh by love;" but it does not derive its power to justify from the efficacy of that love. It justifies in no other way than as it introduces us into a participation of the righteousness of Christ. Otherwise there would be no force in the argument so strenuously urged by the apostle. "To him that worketh," says he, "is the reward not reckoned of grace, but of debt. But to him that worketh not, but believeth on him that justifieth the ungodly, his faith is counted for righteousness." Was it possible for him to speak more plainly than by thus asserting, that there is no righteousness of faith, except where there are no works entitled to any reward; and that faith is imputed for righteousness, only when righteousness is conferred through unmerited grace?

XXI. Now, let us examine the truth of what has been asserted in the definition, that the righteousness of faith is a reconciliation with God, which consists solely in remission of sins. We must always return to this axiom—That the Divine wrath remains on all men, as long as they continue to be sinners. This Isaiah has beautifully expressed in the following words: "The Lord's hand is not shortened, that it cannot save; neither is his ear heavy, that it cannot hear; but your iniquities have separated between you and your God, and your sins have hid his face from you, that he will not hear." We are informed, that sin makes a division between man and God, and turns the Divine countenance away from the sinner. Nor can it be otherwise; because it is incompatible with his righteousness to have any communion with sin. Hence the apostle teaches, that man is an enemy to God, till he be reconciled to him through Christ. Whom, therefore, the Lord receives into fellowship, him he is said to justify; because he cannot receive any one into favour or into fellowship with himself, without making him from a sinner to be a righteous person. This, we add, is accomplished by the remission of sins. For if they, whom the Lord has reconciled to himself, be judged according to their works, they will still be found actually sinners; who, notwithstanding, must be absolved and free from sin. It appears, then, that those whom God receives, are made righteous no otherwise than as they are purified by being cleansed from all their defilements by the remission of their sins; so that such a righteousness may, in one word, be denominated a remission of sins.

XXII. Both these points are fully established by the language of Paul, which I have already recited. "God was in Christ, reconciling the world unto himself, not imputing their trespasses unto them; and hath committed unto us the word of reconciliation." Then he adds the substance of his ministry: "He hath made him to be sin for us, who knew no sin; that we might be made the righteousness of God in him." The terms "righteousness" and "reconciliation" are here used by him indiscriminately, to teach us that they are mutually comprehended in each other. And he states the manner of obtaining this righteousness to consist in our transgressions not being imputed to us. Wherefore we can no longer doubt how God justifies, when we hear that he reconciles us to himself by not imputing our sins to us. Thus, in the Epistle to the Romans, the apostle proves, that "God imputeth righteousness without works," from the testimony of David, who declares, "Blessed are they whose iniquities are forgiven, and whose sins are covered. Blessed is the man to whom the Lord will not impute sin." By "blessedness," in this passage, he undoubtedly means righteousness; for since he asserts it to consist in remission of sins, there is no reason for our adopting any other definition of it. Wherefore Zachariah, the father of John the Baptist, places "the knowledge of salvation" in "the remission of sins." And Paul, observing the same rule in the sermon which he preached to the people of Antioch on the subject of salvation, is stated by Luke to have concluded in the following manner: "Through this man is preached unto you the forgiveness of sins; and by him all that believe are justified from all things, from which ye could not be justified by the law of Moses." The apostle thus connects "forgiveness of sins" with "justification," to show that they are identically the same; whence he justly argues, that this righteousness which we obtain through the favour of God is gratuitously bestowed upon us. Nor should it be thought a strange expression, that believers are justified before God, not by their works, but by his gracious acceptance of them; since it occurs so frequently in the Scripture, and sometimes also in the fathers. Augustine says, "The righteousness of the saints, in this world, consists rather in the remission of their sins than in the perfection of their virtues." With which corresponds the remarkable observation of Bernard: "Not to sin at all, is the righteousness of God; but the righteousness of man is the Divine grace and mercy." He had before asserted, "that Christ is righteousness to us in absolution, and therefore that they alone are righteous who have obtained pardon through his mercy."

XXIII. Hence, also, it is evident, that we obtain justification before God, solely by the intervention of the righteousness of Christ. Which is equivalent to saying, that a man is righteous, not in himself, but because the righteousness of Christ is communicated to him by imputation; and this is a point which deserves an attentive consideration. For it supersedes that idle notion, that a man is justified by faith, because faith receives the Spirit of God by whom he is made righteous; which is too repugnant to the foregoing doctrine, ever to be reconcilable to it. For he must certainly be destitute of all righteousness of his own, who is taught to seek a righteousness out of himself. This is most clearly asserted by the apostle, when he says, "He hath made him to be sin for us, who knew no sin; that we might be made the righteousness of God in him." We see that our righteousness is not in ourselves, but in Christ; and that all our title to it rests solely on our being partakers of Christ; for in possessing him, we possess all his riches with him. Nor does any objection arise from what he states in another place, that "God, sending his own Son in the likeness of sinful flesh, and for sin, condemned sin in the flesh; that the righteousness of the law might be fulfilled in us;" where he intends no other fulfilment than what we obtain by imputation. For the Lord Christ so communicates his righteousness to us, that, with reference to the Divine judgment, he transfuses its virtue into us in a most wonderful manner. That the apostle intended no other, abundantly appears from another declaration, which he had made just before: "As by one man's disobedience many were made sinners, so by the obedience of one shall many be made righteous." What is placing our righteousness in the obedience of Christ, but asserting, that we are accounted righteous only because his obedience is accepted for us as if it were our own? Wherefore Ambrose appears to me to have very beautifully exemplified this righteousness in the benediction of Jacob; that as he, who had on his own account no claim to the privileges of primogeniture, being concealed in his brother's habit, and invested with his garment, which diffused a most excellent odour, insinuated himself into the favour of his father, that he might receive the benediction to his own advantage, under the character of another; so we shelter ourselves under the precious purity of Christ our elder brother, that we may obtain the testimony of righteousness in the sight of God. The words of Ambrose are, "That Isaac smelled the odour of the garments, perhaps indicates, that we are justified not by works, but by faith; since the infirmity of the flesh is an impediment to works, but the brightness of faith, which merits the pardon of sin, conceals the error of our actions." And such is indeed the real fact; for that we may appear before the face of God to salvation, it is necessary for us to be perfumed with his fragrance, and to have all our deformities concealed and absorbed in his perfection.

II. A Consideration of The Divine Tribunal, Necessary to a Serious Conviction of Gratuitous Justification.

Though it appears, from the plainest testimonies, that all these things are strictly true, yet we shall not clearly discover how necessary they are, till we shall have taken a view of what ought to be the foundation of all this argument. In the first place, therefore, we should reflect that we are not treating of the righteousness of a human court, but of that of the heavenly tribunal; in order that we may not apply any diminutive standard of our own, to estimate the integrity of conduct required to satisfy the Divine justice. But it is wonderful, with what temerity and presumption this is commonly decided; and it is even observable, that no men give us more confident or pompous declamations concerning the righteousness of works, than those who are notoriously guilty of open sins or addicted to secret vices. This arises from their never thinking of the righteousness of God, the smallest sense of which would prevent them from treating it with such contempt. And certainly it is exceedingly undervalued, if it be not acknowledged to be so perfect that nothing can be acceptable to it but what is absolutely complete and immaculate, such as it never was, nor ever will be, possible to find in fallen man. It is easy for any one in the cloisters of the schools, to indulge himself in idle speculations on the merit of works to justify men; but when he comes into the presence of God, he must bid farewell to these amusements, for there the business is transacted with seriousness, and no ludicrous logomachy practised. To this point, then, must our attention be directed, if we wish to make any useful inquiry concerning true righteousness; how we can answer the celestial Judge, when he shall call us to an account. Let us place that Judge before our eyes, not according to the spontaneous imaginations of our minds, but according to the descriptions given of him in the Scripture; which represents him as one whose refulgence eclipses the stars, whose power melts the mountains, whose anger shakes the earth, whose wisdom takes the subtle in their own craftiness, whose purity makes all things appear polluted, whose righteousness even the angels are unable to bear, who acquits not the guilty, whose vengeance, when it is once kindled, penetrates even to the abyss of hell. Let him seat himself, I say, on the tribunal, to examine the actions of men: who will present himself fearless before his throne? "Who shall dwell with the devouring fire?" saith the prophet. "Who shall dwell with everlasting burnings? He that walketh righteously and speaketh uprightly," &c. Now let him come forward, whoever he is. But this answer causes not one to appear. For, on the contrary, we hear this fearful speech, "If thou, Lord, shouldst mark iniquities, O Lord, who shall stand?" In truth, all must speedily perish, as it is written in another place, "Shall mortal man be more just than God? Shall a man be more pure than his Maker? Behold, he put no trust in his servants; and his angels he charged with folly; how much less in them that dwell in houses of clay, whose foundation is in the dust, which are crushed before the moth? They are destroyed from morning to evening." Again: "Behold, he putteth no trust in his saints; yea, the heavens are not clean in his sight; how much more abominable and filthy is man, which drinketh iniquity like water?" I confess that in the Book of Job mention is made of a righteousness which is superior to the observance of the law. And it will be of use to remember this distinction; because, though any one could satisfy the law, he could not even then stand the scrutiny of that righteousness which exceeds all comprehension. Therefore, though Job is conscious of his own integrity, yet he is mute with astonishment, when he sees that God could not be pleased even with the sanctity of angels, if he were to enter into a strict examination of their works. I shall, therefore, now pass over that righteousness to which I have alluded, because it is incomprehensible, and content myself with asserting, that we must be worse than stupid, if, on an examination of our lives by the rule of the written law, we are not tormented with awful dread in consequence of so many maledictions, which God has designed to arouse us, and among the rest this general one: "Cursed be he that confirmeth not all the words of this law to do them." In short, this whole controversy will be uninteresting and useless, unless every one present himself as a criminal before the celestial Judge, and voluntarily prostrate and humble himself in deep solicitude concerning his absolution.

II. To this point our eyes ought to have been raised, that we might learn rather to tremble through fear, than to indulge in vain exultation. It is easy, indeed, while the comparison is made only between men, for every man to imagine himself to be possessed of something which others ought not to contemn; but when we ascend to the contemplation of God, that confidence is immediately lost. And the case of our soul with respect to God is similar to that of our body with respect to the visible heavens; for the eye, as long as it is employed in beholding adjacent objects, receives proofs of its own perspicacity; but if it be directed towards the sun, dazzled and confounded with his overpowering brightness, it feels no less debility in beholding him, than strength in the view of inferior objects. Let us not, then, deceive ourselves with a vain confidence, although we consider ourselves equal or superior to other men. That is nothing to God, to whose decision this cause must be submitted. But if our insolence cannot be restrained by these admonitions, he will reply to us in the language which he addressed to the Pharisees: "Ye are they which justify yourselves before men; but that which is highly esteemed among men, is abomination in the sight of God." Go now, and among men proudly glory in your righteousness, while the God of heaven abominates it. But what is the language of the servants of God, who are truly taught by his Spirit? One says, "Enter not into judgment with thy servant; for in thy sight shall no man living be justified." And another, though in a sense somewhat different, "How should man be just with God? If he will contend with him, he cannot answer him one of a thousand." Here we are plainly informed respecting the righteousness of God, that it is such as no human works can satisfy; and such as renders it impossible for us, if accused of a thousand crimes, to exculpate ourselves from one of them. The same idea of this righteousness had very properly been entertained by Paul, that "chosen vessel" of God, when he professed, "I am conscious to myself of nothing; yet am I not hereby justified."

III. Nor is it only in the sacred Scriptures that such examples are found. All pious writers discover similar sentiments. Thus Augustine says, "The only hope of all the pious, who groan under this burden of corruptible flesh, and amidst the infirmities of this life, is, that we have a Mediator, Jesus Christ the righteous; and he is the propitiation for our sins." What is the meaning of this observation? If this is their only hope, where is any confidence in works? For when he asserts this to be the only one, he precludes every other. Bernard also says, "And in fact where can be found safe and solid rest and security for the weak, but in the wounds of the Saviour? There I dwell with the greater security, in proportion to his power to save. The world rages, the body oppresses, the devil lies in wait to destroy. I do not fall, because my foundation is on a firm rock. I have committed heinous sin. My conscience is disturbed, but shall not fall into despair, because I shall recall to remembrance the wounds of the Lord." From these considerations he afterwards concludes, "My merit, therefore, is the compassion of the Lord: I am clearly not destitute of merit, as long as he is not destitute of compassions. But if the mercies of the Lord be a multitude of mercies, my merits are likewise equally numerous. Shall I sing of my own righteousness? O Lord, I will remember thy righteousness alone. For it is mine also, since he is made of God righteousness unto me." Again, in another place: "This is the whole merit of man—to fix all his hope on him who saves the whole man." Likewise in another place, retaining peace to himself, and ascribing the glory to God, he says, "To thee let the glory remain undiminished. It is happy for me, if I have peace. The glory I entirely renounce; lest, if I usurp what is not mine, I lose also that which is offered me." In another place he is still more explicit: "Why should the Church be solicitous about merits, while it has a stronger and more secure reason for glorying in the designs of God? You need not inquire on account of what merits we hope for blessings, especially when you read in the prophet, 'Thus saith the Lord God; I do not this for your sakes, but for mine holy name's sake.' It suffices with respect to merit, to know that merits are not sufficient; but as it suffices for merit not to presume on merits, so to be destitute of merits is sufficient cause of condemnation." We must excuse his custom of freely using the word merits for good works. But his ultimate design was to terrify hypocrites, who indulge themselves in a licentious course of sin against the grace of God; as he presently declares: "Happy is the Church which wants neither merits without presumption, nor presumption without merits. It has some ground of presumption, but not merits. It has merits, but in order to deserve, not to presume. Is not the absence of presumption itself a merit? Therefore the Church presumes the more securely, because it does not presume, having ample cause for glorying in the multitude of the Divine mercies."

IV. This is the real truth. The troubled conscience finds this to be the only asylum of safety, where it can enjoy any tranquillity, when it has to do with the Divine justice. For if the stars, which appeared most brilliant during the night, lose their splendour on the rising of the sun, what can we suppose will be the case with the most excellent innocence of man, when compared with the purity of God? For that will be an examination inconceivably severe, which shall penetrate into all the most secret thoughts of the heart, and, as Paul says, "bring to light the hidden things of darkness, and make manifest the counsels of the hearts;" which shall constrain the reluctant conscience to confess all those things which have now passed away even from our own remembrance. We shall be urged by an accusing devil, who has been privy to all the crimes which he has impelled us to perpetrate. There the external appearance of good works, which now is the sole object of esteem, will be of no avail; sincerity of heart is all that will be required. Wherefore hypocrisy, not only that by which a man, conscious of his guilt before God, affects ostentation before men, but that also by which every man imposes on himself before God, for we are all prone to self-complacency and adulation; hypocrisy in all its forms will then be overwhelmed with confusion, however it may now be intoxicated with presumption and pride. Persons who never look forward to such a spectacle, may, indeed, delightfully and complacently compose for themselves a temporary righteousness, of which they will immediately be stripped at the Divine judgment; just as immense riches, accumulated by us in a dream, vanish as soon as we awake. But they who inquire seriously, and as in the presence of God, respecting the true standard of righteousness, will certainly find that all the actions of men, if estimated according to their intrinsic worth, are utterly defiled and polluted; that what is commonly considered as righteousness, is, in the Divine view, nothing but iniquity; that what is accounted integrity, is mere pollution; and that what is reputed glory, is real ignominy.

V. From this contemplation of the Divine perfection, let us not be unwilling to descend to take a view of ourselves, without adulation or blind self-love. For it is not to be wondered at, if we are so extremely blind in this respect, since not one of us is sufficiently cautious of that pestilent self-indulgence, which the Scripture declares to be naturally inherent in us all. "Every way of man," says Solomon, "is right in his own eyes." Again: "All the ways of a man are clean in his own eyes." But what follows from this? Is he absolved from guilt by this delusion? Not at all; but, as is immediately added, "the Lord weigheth the spirits;" that is, while men are congratulating themselves on account of the external mask of righteousness which they wear, the Lord is at the same time weighing in his own balance the latent impurity of their hearts. Since we are so far from deriving any advantage, therefore, from such blandishments, let us not voluntarily delude ourselves to our own perdition. That we may examine ourselves properly, it is necessary for us to summon our conscience to the tribunal of God. For we have the greatest need of his light in order to detect the recesses of our depravity, which otherwise are too deeply concealed. For then only shall we clearly perceive the force of this language: "How can man be justified with God—man, who is" corruption and "a worm, abominable and filthy, and who drinketh iniquity like water?" "Who can bring a clean thing out of an unclean? Not one." Then also we shall experience what Job said concerning himself: "If I justify myself, mine own mouth shall condemn me; if I say I am perfect, it shall also prove me perverse." For the complaint, which the prophet formerly made respecting Israel, "All we like sheep have gone astray; we have turned every one to his own way;" is applicable not only to one period of time, but to all ages. For he there comprehends all to whom the grace of redemption was to extend; and the rigour of this examination ought to proceed till it shall have filled us with complete consternation, and thus prepared us to receive the grace of Christ. For he is deceived who supposes himself capable of this enjoyment, without having first been truly humbled. It is a well-known observation, that "God resisteth the proud, and giveth grace to the humble."

VI. But what means have we of humbling ourselves, except by submitting, all poor and destitute, to the Divine mercy? For I do not call it humility, if we suppose that we have any thing left. And hitherto they have taught a pernicious hypocrisy, who have connected these two maxims—that we should entertain humble thoughts of ourselves before God, and that we should attach some dignity to our own righteousness. For if we address to God a confession which is contrary to our real sentiments, we are guilty of telling him an impudent falsehood; but we cannot think of ourselves as we ought to think, without utterly despising every thing that may be supposed an excellence in us. When we hear, therefore, from the Psalmist, that "God will save the afflicted people, but will bring down high looks," let us consider, first, that there is no way of salvation till we have laid aside all pride, and attained sincere humility; secondly, that this humility is not a species of modesty, consisting in conceding to God a small portion of what we might justly claim, as they are called humble among men, who neither haughtily exalt themselves nor behave with insolence to others, while they nevertheless entertain some consciousness of excellence: this humility is the unfeigned submission of a mind overwhelmed with a weighty sense of its own misery and poverty; for such is the uniform description of it in the word of God. When the Lord speaks thus in Zephaniah, "I will take away out of the midst of thee them that rejoice in thy pride; I will also leave in the midst of thee an afflicted and poor people, and they shall trust in the name of the Lord;" does he not clearly show who are truly humble? even such as are afflicted with a knowledge of their own poverty. On the contrary, he describes the proud as persons "rejoicing," because this is the usual consequence of prosperity. But to the humble, whom he intends to save, he leaves nothing but that "they trust in the name of the Lord." Thus also in Isaiah, "To this man will I look, even to him that is poor and of a contrite spirit, and trembleth at my word." Again: "Thus saith the high and lofty One that inhabiteth eternity, whose name is Holy; I dwell in the high and holy place, with him also that is of a contrite and humble spirit, to revive the spirit of the humble, and to revive the heart of the contrite ones." By the contrition so frequently mentioned, we must understand a wounded heart, which prevents a man from rising when humbled in the dust. With such contrition must our heart be wounded, if we desire, according to the declaration of the Lord, to be exalted with the humble. If this be not the case, we shall be abased by the powerful hand of God to our shame and disgrace.

VII. And, not content with mere precepts, our excellent Master, in a parable, as in a picture, has presented us with an example of genuine humility. For he introduces a publican, who, "standing afar off, would not lift up so much as his eyes unto heaven, but smote upon his breast, saying, God be merciful to me a sinner." We must not conclude these circumstances—his not presuming to look upwards, standing afar off, smiting upon his breast, and confessing himself a sinner—to be marks of feigned modesty; we may be certain that they were sincere evidences of the disposition of his heart. To him our Lord opposes a Pharisee, who said, "God, I thank thee that I am not as other men are, extortioners, unjust, adulterers, or even as this publican. I fast twice in the week, I give tithes of all that I possess." He openly confesses the righteousness which he has, to be the gift of God; but because he confides in his being righteous, he departs from the presence of God unacceptable and hateful to him. The publican, acknowledging his iniquity, is justified. Hence we may see how very pleasing our humiliation is in the sight of God; so that the heart is not open for the reception of his mercy unless it be divested of all idea of its own dignity. When this notion has occupied the mind, it precludes the admission of Divine mercy. That no one might have any doubt of this, Christ was sent by his Father into the world with a commission, "to preach good tidings unto the meek; to bind up the broken-hearted; to proclaim liberty to the captives, and the opening of the prison to them that are bound; to comfort all that mourn; to give unto them beauty for ashes, the oil of joy for mourning, the garment of praise for the spirit of heaviness." In pursuance of this commission, he invites to a participation of his benefits none but those who "labour and are heavy laden." And in another place he says, "I am not come to call the righteous, but sinners to repentance."

VIII. Therefore, if we would obey the call of Christ, let us dismiss all arrogance and carelessness from our minds. The former arises from a foolish persuasion of our own righteousness, when a man supposes himself to be possessed of any thing, the merit of which can recommend him to God; the latter may exist without any consideration of works. For multitudes of sinners, inebriated with criminal pleasures, and forgetful of the Divine judgment, are in a state, as it were, of lethargic insensibility, so that they never aspire after the mercy which is offered to them. But it is equally necessary for us to shake off such stupidity, and to reject all confidence in ourselves, in order that, being freed from every incumbrance, we may hasten to Christ, all destitute and hungry, to be filled with his blessings. For we shall never have sufficient confidence in him, unless we entirely lose all confidence in ourselves; we shall never find sufficient encouragement in him, unless we are previously dejected in ourselves; we shall never enjoy sufficient consolation in him, unless we are utterly disconsolate in ourselves. We are prepared, therefore, to seek and obtain the grace of God, discarding at the same time all confidence in ourselves, and relying solely on the assurance of his mercy, "when," as Augustine says, "forgetting our own merits, we embrace the free gifts of Christ; because, if he sought merits in us, we should not come to his free gifts." With him Bernard fully agrees, when he compares proud men, that arrogate ever so little to their own merits, to unfaithful servants, because they unjustly claim the praise of the grace which passes through them; just as though a wall should say that it produces the sunbeams which it receives through a window. But not to dwell any longer on this, we may lay it down as a brief, but general and certain maxim, that he is prepared for a participation of the benefits of Divine mercy, who has wholly divested himself, I will not say of his righteousness, which is a mere nullity, but of the vain and airy phantom of righteousness; for as far as any man is satisfied with himself, so far he raises an impediment to the exercise of the grace of God.

III. Two Things Necessary to Be Observed in Gratuitous Justification.

Here are two things to which we must always be particularly attentive; to maintain the glory of the Lord unimpaired and undiminished, and to preserve in our own consciences a placid composure and serene tranquillity with regard to the Divine judgment. We see how frequently and solicitously the Scripture exhorts us to render ascriptions of praise to God alone, when it treats of justification. And, indeed, the apostle assures us that the design of the Lord in conferring righteousness upon us in Christ, is to manifest his own righteousness. The nature of that manifestation he immediately subjoins: it is, "that he might be just, and the justifier of him which believeth in Jesus." The righteousness of God, we see, is not sufficiently illustrious, unless he alone be esteemed righteous, and communicate the grace of justification to the unworthy. For this reason it is his will "that every mouth be stopped, and all the world become guilty before him;" because, as long as man has any thing to allege in his own defence, it detracts something from the glory of God. Thus in Ezekiel he teaches us how greatly we glorify his name by an acknowledgment of our iniquity: "Ye shall remember your ways, (saith he,) and all your doings, wherein ye have been defiled; and ye shall loathe yourselves in your own sight for all your evils that ye have committed. And ye shall know that I am the Lord, when I have wrought with you for my name's sake, not according to your wicked ways, nor according to your corrupt doings." If these things are contained in the true knowledge of God, that, humbled with a consciousness of our iniquity, we should consider him as indulging us with blessings of which we are unworthy, why do we attempt, to our own serious injury, to pilfer the smallest particle of the praise due to his gratuitous goodness? Thus also when Jeremiah proclaims, "Let not the wise man glory in his wisdom, neither let the mighty man glory in his might, let not the rich man glory in his riches; but let him that glorieth glory in the Lord;" does he not suggest that the glory of God sustains some diminution, if any man glory in himself? To this use these words are clearly applied by Paul, when he states, that all the branches of our salvation are deposited with Christ, that we may not glory except in the Lord. For he intimates, that they who suppose themselves to have even the least ground for glorying in themselves, are guilty of rebelling against God, and obscuring his glory.

II. The truth, then, is, that we never truly glory in him, till we have entirely renounced all glory of our own. On the converse, this may be admitted as an axiom universally true, that they who glory in themselves, glory in opposition to God. For Paul is of opinion that the world is not "subject to the judgment of God," till men are deprived of all foundation for glorying. Therefore Isaiah, when he announces, that "in the Lord shall all the seed of Israel be justified," adds also, "and shall glory;" as though he had said, that the end of God in justifying the elect was, that they might glory in himself, and in no other. But how we should glory in the Lord, he had stated in the preceding verse: "Surely, shall one say, in the Lord have I righteousness and strength." Let us observe, that what is required is not a simple confession, but a confession confirmed by an oath; that we may not suppose any fictitious pretence of humility to be sufficient. Here let no one plead that he does not glory at all, when without arrogance he recognizes his own righteousness; for such an opinion cannot exist without generating confidence, nor confidence without being attended with glorying. Let us remember, therefore, in the whole controversy concerning righteousness, that this end must be kept in view, that all the praise of it may remain perfect and undiminished with the Lord; because, according to the apostle's testimony, he has bestowed his grace on us in order "to declare his righteousness; that he might be just, and the justifier of him which believeth in Jesus." Wherefore, in another place, after having declared that the Lord has conferred salvation on us in order to display "the praise of the glory of his grace," repeating, as it were, the same sentiment, he adds, "By grace are ye saved through faith; and that not of yourselves; it is the gift of God; not of works, lest any man should boast." And when Peter admonishes us that we are called to the hope of salvation, "that we should show forth the praises (or virtues) of him who hath called us out of darkness into his marvellous light," he evidently means that the praises of God alone should resound in the ears of believers, so as to impose total silence on all the presumption of the flesh. The conclusion of the whole is, that man cannot without sacrilege arrogate to himself the least particle of righteousness, because it is so much detracted and diminished from the glory of the righteousness of God.

III. Now, if we inquire by what means the conscience can obtain peace before God, we shall find no other than our reception of gratuitous righteousness from his free gift. Let us always remember the inquiry of Solomon—"Who can say, I have made my heart clean, I am pure from my sin?" It is certain that there is no man who is not covered with infinite pollution. Let a man of the most perfect character, then, retire into his own conscience, and enter into a scrutiny of his actions, and what will be the result? Will he feel a high degree of satisfaction, as though there were the most entire agreement between God and him? or will he not rather be lacerated with terrible agonies, on perceiving in himself such ample cause for condemnation, if he be judged according to his works? If the conscience reflect on God, it must either enjoy a solid peace with his judgment, or be surrounded with the terrors of hell. We gain nothing, therefore, in our discussions of this point, unless we establish a righteousness, the stability of which will support our souls under the scrutiny of the Divine judgment. When our souls shall possess what will enable them to appear with boldness in the presence of God, and to await and receive his judgment without any fear, then, and not before, we may be assured that we have found a righteousness which truly deserves the name. It is not without reason, therefore, that this subject is so largely insisted on by the apostle, whose words I prefer to my own: "For if they which are of the law be heirs, faith is made void, and the promise is made of none effect." He first infers, that faith is annulled and superseded, if the promise of righteousness respect the merit of our works, or depend on our observance of the law. For no man could ever securely rely on it, since he never would be able to determine with certainty for himself that he had fulfilled the law, as in fact no man ever does completely satisfy it by any works of his own. Not to seek far for testimonies of this fact, every individual may be his own witness of it, who will enter unprejudiced into an examination of himself. And hence it appears in what deep and dark recesses hypocrisy buries the minds of men, while they indulge themselves in such great security, and hesitate not to oppose their self-adulation to the judgment of God, as though they would stop the proceedings of his tribunal. But believers, who sincerely examine themselves, are troubled and distressed with a solicitude of a very different nature. The minds of men universally, therefore, ought to feel first hesitation, and then despair, while considering, every one for himself, the magnitude of the debt with which they are still oppressed, and their immense distance from the conditions prescribed to them. Behold their confidence already broken and extinguished; for to confide is not to fluctuate, to vary, to be hurried hither and thither, to hesitate, to be kept in suspense, to stagger, and finally to despair; but it is, to strengthen the mind with content, certainty, and solid security, and to have somewhat upon which to stand and to rest.

IV. He adds likewise another consideration, that the promise would be void and of none effect. For if the fulfilment of it depend on our merit, when shall we have made such a progress as to deserve the favour of God? Besides, this second argument is a consequence of the former, since the promise will be fulfilled to those alone who shall exercise faith in it. Therefore, if faith be wanting, the promise will retain no force. "Therefore the inheritance is of faith, that it might be by grace; to the end the promise might be sure to all the seed." For it is abundantly confirmed, when it depends solely on the Divine mercy; because mercy and truth are connected by an indissoluble bond, and whatever God mercifully promises, he also faithfully performs. Thus David, before he implores salvation for himself according to the word of God, first represents it as originating in his mercy: "According to thy word unto thy servant, let thy tender mercies come unto me, that I may live." And for this there is sufficient reason, since God has no other inducement to promise than what arises from his mere mercy. Here, then, we must place, and, as it were, deeply fix, all our hopes, without regarding our own works, or seeking any assistance from them. Nor must it be supposed that we are advancing a new doctrine, for the same conduct is recommended by Augustine. "Christ," says he, "will reign in his servants for ever. God has promised this, God has said it; if that be insufficient, God has sworn it. Since the promise, therefore, is established, not according to our merits, but according to his mercy, no man ought to speak with anxiety of that which he cannot doubt." Bernard also says, "The disciples of Christ asked, Who can be saved? He replied, With men this is impossible, but not with God. This is all our confidence, this our only consolation, this the whole foundation of our hope. But certain of the possibility, what think we of his will? Who knows whether he deserve love or hatred? Who has known the mind of the Lord, or who has been his counsellor? Here, now, we evidently need faith to help us, and his truth to assist us; that what is concealed from us in the heart of the Father, may be revealed by the Spirit, and that the testimony of the Spirit may persuade our hearts that we are sons of God; that he may persuade us by calling and justifying us freely by faith; in which there is, as it were, an intermediate passage from eternal predestination to future glory." Let us draw the following brief conclusion: The Scripture declares that the promises of God have no efficacy, unless they be embraced by the conscience with a steady confidence; and whenever there is any doubt or uncertainty, it pronounces them to be made void. Again, it asserts that they have no stability if they depend on our works. Either, therefore, we must be for ever destitute of righteousness, or our works must not come into consideration, but the ground must be occupied by faith alone, whose nature it is to open the ears and shut the eyes; that is, to be intent only on the promise, and to avert the thoughts from all human dignity or merit. Thus is accomplished that remarkable prophecy of Zechariah: "I will remove the iniquity of that land in one day. In that day, saith the Lord of hosts, shall ye call every man his neighbour under the vine and under the fig-tree;" in which the prophet suggests that believers enjoy no true peace till after they have obtained the remission of their sins. For this analogy must be observed in the prophets, that when they treat of the kingdom of Christ, they exhibit the external bounties of God as figures of spiritual blessings. Wherefore also Christ is denominated "the Prince of peace," and "our Peace;" because he calms all the agitations of the conscience. If we inquire, by what means; we must come to the sacrifice by which God is appeased. For no man will ever lose his fears who shall not be assured that God is propitiated solely by that atonement which Christ has made by sustaining his wrath. In short, we must seek for peace only in the terrors of Christ our Redeemer.

V. But why do I use such an obscure testimony? Paul invariably denies that peace or tranquillity can be enjoyed in the conscience, without a certainty that we are justified by faith. And he also declares whence that certainty proceeds; it is "because the love of God is shed abroad in our hearts by the Holy Ghost;" as though he had said that our consciences can never be satisfied without a certain persuasion of our acceptance with God. Hence he exclaims in the name of all believers, "Who shall separate us from the love of God which is in Christ?" For till we have reached that port of safety, we shall tremble with alarm at every slightest breeze; but while God shall manifest himself as our Shepherd, we shall fear no evil even in the valley of the shadow of death. Whoever they are, therefore, who pretend that we are justified by faith, because, being regenerated, we are righteous by living a spiritual life, they have never tasted the sweetness of grace, so as to have confidence that God would be propitious to them. Whence also it follows, that they know no more of the method of praying aright, than the Turks or any other profane nations. For according to the testimony of Paul, faith is not genuine unless it dictate and suggest that most delightful name of Father, and unless it open our mouth freely to cry, "Abba, Father;" which he in another place expresses still more clearly: "In Christ we have boldness and access with confidence by the faith of him." This certainly arises not from the gift of regeneration; which, being always imperfect in the present state, contains in itself abundant occasion of doubting. Wherefore it is necessary to come to this remedy; that believers should conclude that they cannot hope for an inheritance in the kingdom of heaven on any other foundation, but because, being ingrafted into the body of Christ, they are gratuitously accounted righteous. For with respect to justification, faith is a thing merely passive, bringing nothing of our own to conciliate the favour of God, but receiving what we need from Christ.

IV. The Commencement and Continual Progress of Justification.

For the further elucidation of this subject, let us examine what kind of righteousness can be found in men during the whole course of their lives. Let us divide them into four classes. For either they are destitute of the knowledge of God, and immerged in idolatry; or, having been initiated by the sacraments, they lead impure lives, denying God in their actions, while they confess him with their lips, and belong to Christ only in name; or they are hypocrites, concealing the iniquity of their hearts with vain disguises; or, being regenerated by the Spirit of God, they devote themselves to true holiness. In the first of these classes, judged of according to their natural characters, from the crown of the head to the sole of the foot there will not be found a single spark of goodness; unless we mean to charge the Scripture with falsehood in these representations which it gives of all the sons of Adam—that "the heart is deceitful above all things, and desperately wicked;" that "every imagination of man's heart is evil from his youth;" that "the thoughts of man are vanity; that there is no fear of God before his eyes;" that "there is none that understandeth, none that seeketh after God;" in a word, "that he is flesh," a term expressive of all those works which are enumerated by Paul—"adultery, fornication, uncleanness, lasciviousness, idolatry, witchcraft, hatred, variance, emulations, wrath, strife, seditions, heresies, envyings, murders," and every impurity and abomination that can be conceived. This is the dignity, in the confidence of which they must glory. But if any among them discover that integrity in their conduct which among men has some appearance of sanctity, yet, since we know that God regards not external splendour, we must penetrate to the secret springs of these actions, if we wish them to avail any thing to justification. We must narrowly examine, I say, from what disposition of heart these works proceed. Though a most extensive field of observation is now before us, yet, since the subject may be despatched in very few words, I shall be as compendious as possible.

II. In the first place, I do not deny, that whatever excellences appear in unbelievers, they are the gifts of God. I am not so at variance with the common opinion of mankind, as to contend that there is no difference between the justice, moderation, and equity of Titus or Trajan, and the rage, intemperance, and cruelty of Caligula, or Nero, or Domitian; between the obscenities of Tiberius and the continence of Vespasian; and, not to dwell on particular virtues or vices, between the observance and the contempt of moral obligation and positive laws. For so great is the difference between just and unjust, that it is visible even in the lifeless image of it. For what order will be left in the world, if these opposites be confounded together? Such a distinction as this, therefore, between virtuous and vicious actions, has not only been engraven by the Lord in the heart of every man, but has also been frequently confirmed by his providential dispensations. We see how he confers many blessings of the present life on those who practise virtue among men. Not that this external resemblance of virtue merits the least favour from him; but he is pleased to discover his great esteem of true righteousness, by not permitting that which is external and hypocritical to remain without a temporal reward. Whence it follows, as we have just acknowledged, that these virtues, whatever they may be, or rather images of virtues, are the gifts of God; since there is nothing in any respect laudable which does not proceed from him.

III. Nevertheless the observation of Augustine is strictly true—that all who are strangers to the religion of the one true God, however they may be esteemed worthy of admiration for their reputed virtue, not only merit no reward, but are rather deserving of punishment, because they contaminate the pure gifts of God with the pollution of their own hearts. For though they are instruments used by God for the preservation of human society, by the exercise of justice, continence, friendship, temperance, fortitude, and prudence, yet they perform these good works of God very improperly; being restrained from the commission of evil, not by a sincere attachment to true virtue, but either by mere ambition, or by self-love, or by some other irregular disposition. These actions, therefore, being corrupted in their very source by the impurity of their hearts, are no more entitled to be classed among virtues, than those vices which commonly deceive mankind by their affinity and similitude to virtues. Besides, when we remember that the end of what is right is always to serve God, whatever is directed to any other end, can have no claim to that appellation. Therefore, since they regard not the end prescribed by Divine wisdom, though an act performed by them be externally and apparently good, yet, being directed to a wrong end, it becomes sin. He concludes, therefore, that all the Fabricii, Scipios, and Catos, in all their celebrated actions, were guilty of sin, inasmuch as, being destitute of the light of faith, they did not direct those actions to that end to which they ought to have directed them; that consequently they had no genuine righteousness; because moral duties are estimated not by external actions, but by the ends for which such actions are designed.

IV. Besides, if there be any truth in the assertion of John, that "he that hath not the Son of God, hath not life;" they who have no interest in Christ, whatever be their characters, their actions, or their endeavours, are constantly advancing, through the whole course of their lives, towards destruction and the sentence of eternal death. On this argument is founded the following observation of Augustine: "Our religion discriminates between the righteous and the unrighteous, not by the law of works, but by that of faith, without which works apparently good are perverted into sins." Wherefore the same writer, in another place, strikingly compares the exertions of such men to a deviation in a race from the prescribed course. For the more vigorously any one runs out of the way, he recedes so much the further from the goal, and becomes so much the more unfortunate. Wherefore he contends, that it is better to halt in the way, than to run out of the way. Finally, it is evident that they are evil trees, since without a participation of Christ there is no sanctification. They may produce fruits fair and beautiful to the eye, and even sweet to the taste, but never any that are good. Hence we clearly perceive that all the thoughts, meditations, and actions of man, antecedent to a reconciliation to God by faith, are accursed, and not only of no avail to justification, but certainly deserving of condemnation. But why do we dispute concerning it as a dubious point, when it is already proved by the testimony of the apostle, that "without faith it is impossible to please God?"

V. But the proof will be still clearer, if the grace of God be directly opposed to the natural condition of man. The Scripture invariably proclaims, that God finds nothing in men which can incite him to bless them, but that he prevents them by his gratuitous goodness. For what can a dead man do to recover life? But when God illuminates us with the knowledge of himself, he is said to raise us from death, and to make us new creatures. For under this character we find the Divine goodness towards us frequently celebrated, especially by the apostle. "God," says he, "who is rich in mercy, for his great love wherewith he loved us, even when we were dead in sins, hath quickened us together with Christ," &c. In another place, when, under the type of Abraham, he treats of the general calling of believers, he says, It is "God, who quickeneth the dead, and calleth those things which be not as though they were." If we are nothing, what can we do? Wherefore God forcibly represses this presumption, in the Book of Job, in the following words: "Who hath prevented me, that I should repay him? Whatsoever is under the whole heaven is mine." Paul, explaining this passage, concludes from it, that we ought not to suppose we bring any thing to the Lord but ignominious indigence and emptiness. Wherefore, in the passage cited above, in order to prove that we attain to the hope of salvation, not by works, but solely by the grace of God, he alleges, that "we are his workmanship, created in Christ Jesus unto good works, which God hath before ordained that we should walk in them." As though he would say, Who of us can boast that he has influenced God by his righteousness, since our first power to do well proceeds from regeneration? For, according to the constitution of our nature, oil might be extracted from a stone sooner than we could perform a good work. It is wonderful, indeed, that man, condemned to such ignominy, dares to pretend to have any thing left. Let us confess, therefore, with that eminent servant of the Lord, that "God hath saved us, and called us with a holy calling, not according to our works, but according to his own purpose and grace;" and that "the kindness and love of God our Saviour towards man appeared," because "not by works of righteousness which we have done, but according to his mercy he saved us; that being justified by his grace, we should be made heirs of eternal life." By this confession we divest man of all righteousness, even to the smallest particle, till through mere mercy he has been regenerated to the hope of eternal life; for if a righteousness of works contributed any thing to our justification, we are not truly said to be "justified by grace." The apostle, when he asserted justification to be by grace, had certainly not forgotten his argument in another place, that "if it be of works, then it is no more grace." And what else does our Lord intend, when he declares, "I am not come to call the righteous, but sinners?" If sinners only are admitted, why do we seek to enter by a counterfeit righteousness?

VI. The same thought frequently recurs to me, that I am in danger of injuring the mercy of God, by labouring with so much anxiety in the defence of this doctrine, as though it were doubtful or obscure. But such being our malignity, that, unless it be most powerfully subdued, it never allows to God that which belongs to him, I am constrained to dwell a little longer upon it. But as the Scripture is sufficiently perspicuous on this subject, I shall use its language in preference to my own. Isaiah, after having described the universal ruin of mankind, properly subjoins the method of recovery. "The Lord saw it, and it displeased him that there was no judgment. And he saw that there was no man, and wondered that there was no intercessor: therefore his own arm brought salvation unto him; and his righteousness it sustained him." Where are our righteousnesses, if it be true, as the prophet says, that no one assists the Lord in procuring his salvation? So another prophet introduces the Lord speaking of the reconciliation of sinners to himself, saying, "I will betroth thee unto me for ever, in righteousness, and in judgment, and in loving-kindness, and in mercies. I will have mercy upon her that had not obtained mercy." If this covenant, which is evidently our first union with God, depend on his mercy, there remains no foundation for our righteousness. And I should really wish to be informed by those, who pretend that man advances to meet God with some righteousness of works, whether there be any righteousness at all, but that which is accepted by God. If it be madness to entertain such a thought, what that is acceptable to God can proceed from his enemies, who, with all their actions, are the objects of his complete abhorrence? And that we are all the inveterate and avowed enemies of our God, till we are justified and received into his friendship, is an undeniable truth. If justification be the principle from which love originates, what righteousnesses of works can precede it? To destroy that pestilent arrogance, therefore, John carefully apprizes us that "we did not first love him." And the Lord had by his prophet long before taught the same truth: "I will love them freely," saith he, "for mine anger is turned away." If his love was spontaneously inclined towards us, it certainly is not excited by works. But the ignorant mass of mankind have only this notion of it—that no man has merited that Christ should effect our redemption; but that towards obtaining the possession of redemption, we derive some assistance from our own works. But however we may have been redeemed by Christ, yet till we are introduced into communion with him by the calling of the Father, we are both heirs of darkness and death, and enemies to God. For Paul teaches, that we are not purified and washed from our pollutions by the blood of Christ, till the Spirit effects that purification within us. This is the same that Peter intends, when he declares that the "sanctification of the Spirit" is effectual "unto obedience, and sprinkling of the blood of Jesus Christ." If we are sprinkled by the Spirit with the blood of Christ for purification, we must not imagine that before this ablution we are in any other state than that of sinners destitute of Christ. We may be certain, therefore, that the commencement of our salvation is, as it were, a resurrection from death to life; because, when "on the behalf of Christ it is given to us to believe on him," we then begin to experience a transition from death to life.

VII. The same reasoning may be applied to the second and third classes of men in the division stated above. For the impurity of the conscience proves, that they are neither of them yet regenerated by the Spirit of God; and their unregeneracy betrays also their want of faith: whence it appears, that they are not yet reconciled to God, or justified in his sight, since these blessings are only attained by faith. What can be performed by sinners alienated from God, that is not execrable in his view? Yet all the impious, and especially hypocrites, are inflated with this foolish confidence. Though they know that their heart is full of impurity, yet if they perform any specious actions, they esteem them too good to be despised by God. Hence that pernicious error, that though convicted of a polluted and impious heart, they cannot be brought to confess themselves destitute of righteousness; but while they acknowledge themselves to be unrighteous, because it cannot be denied, they still arrogate to themselves some degree of righteousness. This vanity the Lord excellently refutes by the prophet. "Ask now," saith he, "the priests, saying, If one bear holy flesh in the skirt of his garment, and with his skirt do touch bread, or any meat, shall it be holy? And the priests answered and said, No. Then said Haggai, If one that is unclean by a dead body touch any of these, shall it be unclean? And the priests answered and said, It shall be unclean. Then answered Haggai, and said, So is this people, and so is this nation before me, saith the Lord; and so is every work of their hands; and that which they offer there is unclean." I wish that this passage might either obtain full credit with us, or be deeply impressed on our memory. For there is no one, however flagitious his whole life may be, who can suffer himself to be persuaded of what the Lord here plainly declares. The greatest sinner, as soon as he has performed two or three duties of the law, doubts not but they are accepted of him for righteousness; but the Lord positively denies that any sanctification is acquired by such actions, unless the heart be previously well purified; and not content with this, he asserts that all the works of sinners are contaminated by the impurity of their hearts. Let the name of righteousness, then, no longer be given to these works which are condemned for their pollution by the lips of God. And by what a fine similitude does he demonstrate this! For it might have been objected that what the Lord had enjoined was inviolably holy. But he shows, on the contrary, that it is not to be wondered at, if those things which are sanctified by the law of the Lord, are defiled by the pollution of the wicked; since an unclean hand cannot touch any thing that has been consecrated, without profaning it.

VIII. He excellently pursues the same argument also in Isaiah: "Bring no more vain oblations; incense is an abomination unto me; your new moons and your appointed feasts my soul hateth; they are a trouble unto me; I am weary to bear them. When ye spread forth your hands, I will hide mine eyes from you; yea, when ye make many prayers, I will not hear: your hands are full of blood. Wash you, make you clean; put away the evil of your doings." What is the reason that the Lord is so displeased at an obedience to his law? But, in fact, he here rejects nothing that arises from the genuine observance of the law; the beginning of which, he every where teaches, is an unfeigned fear of his name. If that be wanting, all the oblations made to him are not merely trifles, but nauseous and abominable pollutions. Let hypocrites go now, and, retaining depravity concealed in their hearts, endeavour by their works to merit the favour of God. But by such means they will add provocation to provocation; for "the sacrifice of the wicked is an abomination to the Lord; but the prayer of the upright" alone "is his delight." We lay it down, therefore, as an undoubted truth, which ought to be well known to such as are but moderately versed in the Scriptures, that even the most splendid works of men not yet truly sanctified, are so far from righteousness in the Divine view, that they are accounted sins. And therefore they have strictly adhered to the truth, who have maintained that the works of a man do not conciliate God's favour to his person; but, on the contrary, that works are never acceptable to God, unless the person who performs them has previously found favour in his sight. And this order, to which the Scripture directs us, is religiously to be observed. Moses relates, that "The Lord had respect unto Abel and to his offering." Does he not plainly indicate that the Lord is propitious to men, before he regards their works? Wherefore the purification of the heart is a necessary prerequisite, in order that the works which we perform may be favourably received by God; for the declaration of Jeremiah is always in force, that the "eyes of the Lord are upon the truth." And the Holy Spirit has asserted by the mouth of Peter, that it is "by faith" alone that the "heart" is "purified," which proves that the first foundation is laid in a true and living faith.

IX. Let us now examine what degree of righteousness is possessed by those whom we have ranked in the fourth class. We admit, that when God, by the interposition of the righteousness of Christ, reconciles us to himself, and having granted us the free remission of our sins, esteems us as righteous persons, to this mercy he adds also another blessing; for he dwells in us by his Holy Spirit, by whose power our carnal desires are daily more and more mortified, and we are sanctified, that is, consecrated to the Lord unto real purity of life, having our hearts moulded to obey his law, so that it is our prevailing inclination to submit to his will, and to promote his glory alone by all possible means. But even while, under the guidance of the Holy Spirit, we are walking in the ways of the Lord,—that we may not forget ourselves, and be filled with pride, we feel such remains of imperfection, as afford us abundant cause for humility. The Scripture declares, that "there is not a just man upon earth, that doeth good and sinneth not." What kind of righteousness, then, will even believers obtain from their own works? In the first place, I assert, that the best of their performances are tarnished and corrupted by some carnal impurity and debased by a mixture of some alloy. Let any holy servant of God select from his whole life that which he shall conceive to have been the best of all his actions, and let him examine it with attention on every side; he will undoubtedly discover in it some taint of the corruption of the flesh; since our alacrity to good actions is never what it ought to be, but our course is retarded by great debility. Though we perceive that the blemishes which deform the works of the saints, are not difficult to be discovered, yet suppose we admit them to be very diminutive spots, will they not be at all offensive in the sight of God, in which even the stars are not pure? We have now ascertained, that there is not a single action performed by the saints, which, if judged according to its intrinsic merit, does not justly deserve to be rewarded with shame.

X. In the next place, even though it were possible for us to perform any works completely pure and perfect, yet one sin is sufficient to extinguish and annihilate all remembrance of antecedent righteousness, as is declared by the prophet. With him James also agrees: "Whosoever shall offend," says he, "in one point, he is guilty of all." Now, since this mortal life is never pure or free from sin, whatever righteousness we might acquire being perpetually corrupted, overpowered, and destroyed by subsequent sins, it would neither be admitted in the sight of God, nor be imputed to us for righteousness. Lastly, in considering the righteousness of works, we should regard, not any action commanded in the law, but the commandment itself. Therefore, if we seek righteousness by the law, it is in vain for us to perform two or three works; a perpetual observance of the law is indispensably necessary. Wherefore God does not impute to us for righteousness that remission of sins, of which we have spoken, once only, (as some foolishly imagine,) in order that, having obtained pardon for our past lives, we may afterwards seek righteousness by the law; which would be only sporting with us, and deluding us by a fallacious hope. For since perfection is unattainable by us, as long as we are in this mortal body, and the law denounces death and judgment on all whose works are not completely and universally righteous, it will always have matter of accusation and condemnation against us, unless it be prevented by the Divine mercy continually absolving us by a perpetual remission of our sins. Wherefore it will ever be true, as we asserted at the beginning, that if we be judged according to our demerits, whatever be our designs or undertakings, we are nevertheless with all our endeavours and all our pursuits, deserving of death and destruction.

XI. We must strenuously insist on these two points—first, that there never was an action performed by a pious man, which, if examined by the scrutinizing eye of Divine justice, would not deserve condemnation; and secondly, if any such thing be admitted, (though it cannot be the case with any individual of mankind,) yet being corrupted and contaminated by the sins, of which its performer is confessedly guilty, it loses every claim to the Divine favour. And this is the principal hinge on which our controversy [with the Papists] turns. For concerning the beginning of justification, there is no dispute between us and the sounder schoolmen, but we all agree, that a sinner being freely delivered from condemnation obtains righteousness, and that by the remission of his sins; only they, under the term justification, comprehend that renovation in which we are renewed by the Spirit of God to an obedience to the law, and so they describe the righteousness of a regenerate man as consisting in this—that a man, after having been once reconciled to God through faith in Christ, is accounted righteous with God on account of his good works, the merit of which is the cause of his acceptance. But the Lord, on the contrary, declares, "that faith was reckoned to Abraham for righteousness," not during the time while he yet remained a worshipper of idols, but after he had been eminent during many years for the sanctity of his life. Abraham, then, had for a long time worshipped God from a pure heart, and performed all that obedience to the law, which a mortal man is capable of performing; yet, after all, his righteousness consisted in faith. Whence we conclude, according to the argument of Paul, that it was not of works. So when the prophet says, "The just shall live by his faith," he is not speaking of the impious and profane, whom the Lord justifies by converting them to the faith; but his address is directed to believers, and they are promised life by faith. Paul also removes every doubt, when, in confirmation of this sentiment, he adduces the following passage of David: "Blessed are they whose iniquities are forgiven." But it is certain that David spake not of impious men, but of believers, whose characters resembled his own; for he spoke from the experience of his own conscience. Wherefore it is necessary for us, not to have this blessing for once only, but to retain it as long as we live. Lastly, he asserts, that the message of a free reconciliation with God, is not only promulgated for a day or two, but is perpetual in the church. Believers, therefore, even to the end of their lives, have no other righteousness than that which is there described. For the mediatorial office is perpetually sustained by Christ, by whom the Father is reconciled to us; and the efficacy of whose death is perpetually the same, consisting in ablution, satisfaction, expiation, and perfect obedience, which covers all our iniquities. And Paul does not tell the Ephesians that they are indebted to grace merely for the beginning of their salvation, but that they "are saved by grace, not of works, lest any man should boast."

XII. The subterfuges, by which the schoolmen endeavour to evade these arguments, are unavailing. They say, that the sufficiency of good works to justification arises not from their intrinsic merit, but from the grace through which they are accepted. Secondly, because they are constrained to acknowledge the righteousness of works to be always imperfect in the present state, they admit, that as long as we live we need the remission of our sins, in order to supply the defects of our works; but that our deficiencies are compensated by works of supererogation. I reply, that what they denominate the grace through which our works are accepted, is no other than the free goodness of the Father, with which he embraces us in Christ, when he invests us with the righteousness of Christ, and accepts it as ours, in order that, in consequence of it, he may treat us as holy, pure, and righteous persons. For the righteousness of Christ (which, being the only perfect righteousness, is the only one that can bear the Divine scrutiny) must be produced on our behalf, and judicially presented, as in the case of a surety. Being furnished with this, we obtain by faith the perpetual remission of our sins. Our imperfections and impurities, being concealed by its purity, are not imputed to us, but are as it were buried, and prevented from appearing in the view of Divine justice, till the advent of that hour, when the old man being slain and utterly annihilated in us, the Divine goodness shall receive us into a blessed peace with the new Adam, in that state to wait for the day of the Lord, when we shall receive incorruptible bodies, and be translated to the glories of the celestial kingdom.

XIII. If these things are true, surely no works of ours can render us acceptable to God; nor can the actions themselves be pleasing to him, any otherwise than as a man, who is covered with the righteousness of Christ, pleases God and obtains the remission of his sins. For God has not promised eternal life as a reward of certain works; he only declares, that "he that doeth these things shall live," denouncing, on the contrary, that memorable curse against all who continue not in the observance of every one of his commands. This abundantly refutes the erroneous notion of a partial righteousness, since no other righteousness is admitted into heaven but an entire observance of the law. Nor is there any more solidity in their pretence of a sufficient compensation for imperfections by works of supererogation. For are they not by this perpetually recurring to the subterfuge, from which they have already been driven, that the partial observance of the law constitutes, as far as it goes, a righteousness of works? They unblushingly assume as granted, what no man of sound judgment will concede. The Lord frequently declares, that he acknowledges no righteousness of works, except in a perfect obedience to his law. What presumption is it for us, who are destitute of this, in order that we may not appear to be despoiled of all our glory, or, in other words, to submit entirely to the Lord—what presumption is it for us to boast of I know not what fragments of a few actions, and to endeavour to supply deficiencies by other satisfactions! Satisfactions have already been so completely demolished, that they ought not to occupy even a transient thought. I only remark, that those who trifle in this manner, do not consider what an execrable thing sin is in the sight of God; for indeed they ought to know, that all the righteousness of all mankind, accumulated in one mass, is insufficient to compensate for a single sin. We see that man on account of one offence was rejected and abandoned by God, so that he lost all means of regaining salvation. They are deprived, therefore, of the power of satisfaction, with which, however they flatter themselves, they will certainly never be able to render a satisfaction to God, to whom nothing will be pleasing or acceptable that proceeds from his enemies. Now, his enemies are all those to whom he determines to impute sin. Our sins, therefore, must be covered and forgiven, before the Lord can regard any of our works. Whence it follows that the remission of sins is absolutely gratuitous, and that it is wickedly blasphemed by those who obtrude any satisfactions. Let us, therefore, after the example of the apostle, "forgetting those things which are behind, and reaching forth unto those things which are before, press toward the mark for the prize of our high calling."

XIV. But how is the pretence of works of supererogation consistent with this injunction—"When ye shall have done all those things which are commanded you, say, We are unprofitable servants; we have done that which was our duty to do?" This direction does not inculcate an act of simulation or falsehood, but a decision in our mind respecting that of which we are certain. The Lord, therefore, commands us sincerely to think and consider with ourselves, that our services to him are none of them gratuitous, but merely the performance of indispensable duties; and that justly; for we are servants under such numerous obligations as we could never discharge; even though all our thoughts and all our members were devoted to the duties of the law. In saying, therefore, "When ye shall have done all those things which are commanded," he supposes a case of one man having attained to a degree of righteousness beyond what is attained by all the men in the world. How, then, while every one of us is at the greatest distance from this point, can we presume to glory that we have completely attained to that perfect standard? Nor can any one reasonably object, that there is nothing to prevent his efforts from going beyond his necessary obligations, who in any respect fails of doing the duty incumbent on him. For we must acknowledge, that we cannot imagine any thing pertaining either to the service of God or to the love of our neighbour, which is not comprehended in the Divine law. But if it is a part of the law, let us not boast of voluntary liberality, where we are bound by necessity.

XV. It is irrelevant to this subject, to allege the boasting of Paul, that among the Corinthians he voluntarily receded from what, if he had chosen, he might have claimed as his right, and not only did what was incumbent on him to do, but afforded them his gratuitous services beyond the requisitions of duty. They ought to attend to the reason there assigned, that he acted thus, "lest he should hinder the gospel of Christ." For wicked and fraudulent teachers recommended themselves by this stratagem of liberality, by which they endeavoured, both to conciliate a favourable reception to their own pernicious dogmas, and to fix an odium on the gospel; so that Paul was necessitated either to endanger the doctrine of Christ, or to oppose these artifices. Now, if it be a matter of indifference to a Christian to incur an offence when he may avoid it, I confess that the apostle performed for the Lord a work of supererogation; but if this was justly required of a prudent minister of the gospel, I maintain that he did what was his duty to do. Even if no such reason appeared, yet the observation of Chrysostom is always true—that all that we have is on the same tenure as the possessions of slaves, which the law pronounces to be the property of their masters. And Christ has clearly delivered the same truth in the parable, where he inquires whether we thank a servant, when he returns home in the evening, after the various labours of the day. But it is possible that he may have laboured with greater diligence than we had ventured to require. This may be granted; yet he has done no more than, by the condition of servitude, he was under an obligation to do; since he belongs to us, with all the ability he has. I say nothing of the nature of the supererogations which these men wish to boast of before God; for they are contemptible trifles, which he has never commanded, which he does not approve, nor, when they render up their account to him, will he accept them. We cannot admit that there are any works of supererogation, except such as those of which it is said by the prophet, "Who hath required this at your hand?" But let them remember the language of another passage respecting these things: "Wherefore do ye spend money for that which is not bread? and your labour for that which satisfieth not?" It is easy, indeed, for these idle doctors to dispute concerning these things in easy chairs; but when the Judge of all shall ascend the judgment seat, all such empty notions must vanish away. The object of our inquiries ought to be, what plea we may bring forward with confidence at his tribunal, not what we can invent in schools and cloisters.

XVI. On this subject our minds require to be guarded chiefly against two pernicious principles—That we place no confidence in the righteousness of our works, and that we ascribe no glory to them. The Scriptures every where drive us from all confidence, when they declare that all our righteousnesses are odious in the Divine view, unless they are perfumed with the holiness of Christ; and that they can only excite the vengeance of God, unless they are supported by his merciful pardon. Thus they leave us nothing to do, but to deprecate the wrath of our Judge with the confession of David, "Enter not into judgment with thy servant; for in thy sight shall no man living be justified." And where Job says, "If I be wicked, woe unto me; and if I be righteous, yet will I not lift up my head;" though he refers to that consummate righteousness of God, compared to which even the angels are deficient, yet he at the same time shows, that when God comes to judgment, all men must be dumb. For he not only means that he would rather freely recede, than incur the danger of contending with the rigour of God, but signifies that he experiences in himself no other righteousness than what would instantaneously vanish before the Divine presence. When confidence is destroyed, all boasting must of necessity be relinquished. For who can give the praise of righteousness to his works, in which he is afraid to confide in the presence of God? We must therefore have recourse to the Lord, in whom we are assured, by Isaiah, that "all the seed of Israel shall be justified, and shall glory;" for it is strictly true, as he says in another place, that we are "the planting of the Lord, that he might be glorified." Our minds therefore will then be properly purified, when they shall in no degree confide nor glory in our works. But foolish men are led into such a false and delusive confidence, by the error of always considering their works as the cause of their salvation.

XVII. But if we advert to the four kinds of causes, which the philosophers direct us to consider in the production of effects, we shall find none of them consistent with works in the accomplishment of our salvation. For the Scripture every where proclaims, that the efficient cause of eternal life being procured for us, was the mercy of our heavenly Father, and his gratuitous love towards us; that the material cause is Christ and his obedience, by which he obtained a righteousness for us; and what shall we denominate the formal and instrumental cause, unless it be faith? These three John comprehends in one sentence, when he says, that "God so loved the world that he gave his only begotten Son, that whosoever believeth in him should not perish, but have everlasting life." The final cause the apostle declares to be, both the demonstration of the Divine righteousness and the praise of the Divine goodness, in a passage in which he also expressly mentions the other three causes. For this is his language to the Romans: "All have sinned, and come short of the glory of God, being justified freely by his grace:" here we have the original source of our salvation, which is the gratuitous mercy of God towards us. It follows, "through the redemption that is in Christ Jesus:" here we have the matter of our justification. "Through faith in his blood:" here he points out the instrumental cause, by which the righteousness of Christ is revealed to us. Lastly, he subjoins the end of all, when he says, "To declare his righteousness; that he might be just, and the justifier of him which believeth in Jesus." And to suggest, by the way, that this righteousness consists in reconciliation or propitiation, he expressly asserts that Christ was "set forth to be a propitiation." So also in the first Chapter to the Ephesians, he teaches that we are received into the favour of God through his mere mercy; that it is accomplished by the mediation of Christ; that it is apprehended by faith; and that the end of all is, that the glory of the Divine goodness may be fully displayed. When we see that every part of our salvation is accomplished without us, what reason have we to confide or to glory in our works? Nor can even the most inveterate enemies of Divine grace raise any controversy with us concerning the efficient or the final cause, unless they mean altogether to renounce the authority of the Scripture. Over the material and formal causes they superinduce a false colouring; as if our own works were to share the honour of them with faith and the righteousness of Christ. But this also is contradicted by the Scripture, which affirms that Christ is the sole author of our righteousness and life, and that this blessing of righteousness is enjoyed by faith alone.

XVIII. The saints often confirm and console themselves with the remembrance of their own innocence and integrity, and sometimes even refrain not from proclaiming it. Now, this is done for two reasons; either that, in comparing their good cause with the bad cause of the impious, they derive from such comparison an assurance of victory, not so much by the commendation of their own righteousness, as by the just and merited condemnation of their adversaries; or that, even without any comparison with others, while they examine themselves before God, the purity of their consciences affords them some consolation and confidence. To the former of these reasons we shall advert hereafter; let us now briefly examine the consistency of the latter with what we have before asserted, that in the sight of God we ought to place no reliance on the merit of works, nor glory on account of them. The consistency appears in this—that for the foundation and accomplishment of their salvation, the saints look to the Divine goodness alone, without any regard to works. And they not only apply themselves to it above all things, as the commencement of their happiness, but likewise depend upon it as the consummation of their felicity. A conscience thus founded, built up, and established, is also confirmed by the consideration of works; that is, as far as they are evidences of God dwelling and reigning in us. Now, this confidence of works being found in none but those who have previously cast all the confidence of their souls on the mercy of God, it ought not to be thought contrary to that upon which it depends. Wherefore, when we exclude the confidence of works, we only mean that the mind of a Christian should not be directed to any merit of works as a mean of salvation; but should altogether rely on the gratuitous promise of righteousness. We do not forbid him to support and confirm this faith by marks of the Divine benevolence to him. For if, when we call to remembrance the various gifts which God has conferred on us, they are all as so many rays from the Divine countenance, by which we are illuminated to contemplate the full blaze of supreme goodness,—much more the grace of good works, which demonstrates that we have received the Spirit of adoption.

XIX. When the saints, therefore, confirm their faith, or derive matter of rejoicing from the integrity of their consciences, they only conclude, from the fruits of vocation, that they have been adopted by the Lord as his children. The declaration of Solomon, that "In the fear of the Lord is strong confidence;" and the protestation sometimes used by the saints to obtain a favourable audience from the Lord, that "they have walked before" him "in truth and with a perfect heart;" these things have no concern in laying the foundation for establishing the conscience; nor are they of any value, except as they are consequences of the Divine vocation. For there nowhere exists that fear of God which can establish a full assurance, and the saints are conscious that their integrity is yet accompanied with many relics of corruption. But as the fruits of regeneration evince that the Holy Spirit dwells in them, this affords them ample encouragement to expect the assistance of God in all their necessities, because they experience him to be their Father in an affair of such vast importance. And even this they cannot attain, unless they have first apprehended the Divine goodness, confirmed by no other assurance but that of the promise. For if they begin to estimate it by their good works, nothing will be weaker or more uncertain; for, if their works be estimated in themselves, their imperfection will menace them with the wrath of God, as much as their purity, however incomplete, testifies his benevolence. In a word, they declare the benefits of God, but in such a way as not to turn away from his gratuitous favour, in which Paul assures us there is "length, and breadth, and depth, and height;" as though he had said, Which way soever the pious turn their views, how high soever they ascend, how widely soever they expatiate, yet they ought not to go beyond the love of Christ, but employ themselves wholly in meditating on it, because it comprehends in itself all dimensions. Therefore he says that it "passeth knowledge," and that when we know how much Christ has loved us, we are "filled with all the fulness of God." So also in another place, when he glories that believers are victorious in every conflict, he immediately adds, as the reason of it, "through him that loved us."

XX. We see now, that the confidence which the saints have in their works is not such as either ascribes any thing to the merit of them, (since they view them only as the gifts of God, in which they acknowledge his goodness, and as marks of their calling, whence they infer their election,) or derogates the least from the gratuitous righteousness which we obtain in Christ; since it depends upon it, and cannot subsist without it. This is concisely and beautifully represented by Augustine, when he says, "I do not say to the Lord, Despise not the works of my hands. I have sought the Lord with my hands, and I have not been deceived. But I commend not the works of my hands; for I fear that when thou hast examined them, thou wilt find more sin than merit. This only I say, this I ask, this I desire; Despise not the works of thy hands. Behold in me thy work, not mine. For if thou beholdest mine, thou condemnest me; if thou beholdest thine own, thou crownest me. Because whatever good works I have, they are from thee." He assigns two reasons why he ventured not to boast of his works to God; first, that if he has any good ones, he sees nothing of his own in them; secondly, that even these are buried under a multitude of sins. Hence the conscience experiences more fear and consternation than security. Therefore he desires God to behold his best performances, only that he may recognize in them the grace of his own calling, and perfect the work which he has begun.

XXI. The remaining objection is, that the Scripture represents the good works of believers as the causes for which the Lord blesses them. But this must be understood so as not to affect what we have before proved, that the efficient cause of our salvation is the love of God the Father; the material cause, the obedience of the Son; the instrumental cause, the illumination of the Spirit, that is, faith; and the final cause, the glory of the infinite goodness of God. No obstacle arises from these things to prevent good works being considered by the Lord as inferior causes. But how does this happen? Because those whom his mercy has destined to the inheritance of eternal life, he, in his ordinary dispensations, introduces to the possession of it by good works. That which, in the order of his dispensations, precedes, he denominates the cause of that which follows. For this reason he sometimes deduces eternal life from works; not that the acceptance of it is to be referred to them; but because he justifies the objects of his election, that he may finally glorify them; he makes the former favour, which is a step to the succeeding one, in some sense the cause of it. But whenever the true cause is to be assigned, he does not direct us to take refuge in works, but confines our thoughts entirely to his mercy. For what does he teach us by the apostle? "The wages of sin is death; but the gift of God is eternal life through Jesus Christ our Lord." Why does he not oppose righteousness to sin, as well as life to death? Why does he not make righteousness the cause of life, as well as sin the cause of death? For then the antithesis would have been complete, whereas by this variation it is partly destroyed. But the apostle intended by this comparison to express a certain truth—that death is due to the demerits of men, and that life proceeds solely from the mercy of God. Lastly, these phrases denote rather the order of the Divine gifts, than the cause of them. In the accumulation of graces upon graces, God derives from the former a reason for adding the next, that he may not omit any thing necessary to the enrichment of his servants. And while he thus pursues his liberality, he would have us always to remember his gratuitous election, which is the source and original of all. For although he loves the gifts which he daily confers, as emanations from that fountain, yet it is our duty to adhere to that gratuitous acceptance, which alone can support our souls, and to connect the gifts of his Spirit, which he afterwards bestows on us, with the first cause, in such a manner as will not be derogatory to it.

Note

If you wish to read more of this text, you can find it in Calvin's Institutes of the Christian Religion, Book III.

Enjoyed your Christian reading?

Don't end your introduction to Christian literature here.

Send a blank email to

thegoodchristian10@gmail.com

for access to Christian audiobooks.